THE GOD of
ABRAHAM, ISAAC & JACOB

WATCHMAN NEE

Living Stream Ministry
Anaheim, California • www.lsm.org

First Edition, September 1995.

ISBN 0-87083-932-2

Published by

Living Stream Ministry
2431 W. La Palma Ave., Anaheim, CA 92801 U.S.A.
P. O. Box 2121, Anaheim, CA 92814 U.S.A.

Printed in the United States of America

01 02 03 04 / 12 11 10 9 8 7 6 5 4

CONTENTS

PREFACE

Watchman Nee gave a series of studies on the characters of Abraham, Isaac, and Jacob in the early part of 1940. These messages were published in Chinese in 1955 by the Taiwan Gospel Bookroom under the title, *The God of Abraham, Isaac, and Jacob*. This book is a translation of the Chinese publication.

PREFACE TO THE CHINESE EDITION

God said, "I am...the God of Abraham, the God of Isaac, and the God of Jacob" (Exo. 3:6).

In order to bring a group of people to come under His name, and in order to make them His people, God did a special work in three persons, Abraham, Isaac, and Jacob, respectively, and gave each one of them particular experiences. God gave Abraham the experience of knowing God as the Father, showing that everything comes from God. He gave Isaac the experience of knowing the enjoyment of the Son, showing that everything the Son has is from the Father. He gave Jacob the experience of the discipline of the Holy Spirit to deal with his natural life and constitute Christ into him.

Abraham, Isaac, and Jacob are the beginning of the history of God's people. As such, their total experience should be the experience of all of God's people. In publishing this book, we hope that the readers will find spiritual meaning in the experience of Abraham, Isaac, and Jacob in God's Word. May God bless this book and its readers and guide us to a full knowledge of the God of Abraham, Isaac, and Jacob so that we can become vessels of God's testimony.

The Editors
Taiwan Gospel Book Room
February 1955

CHAPTER ONE

INTRODUCTION

Scripture Reading: Exo. 3:6, 15-16; Matt. 22:31-32

ONE

First Corinthians 10:11 says, "Now these things happened to them as an example...." The Bible records the history of the Israelites as an example to us. It is for the purpose of our edification. Although there is an outward difference between God's work in the Old Testament and His work in the New Testament, they are the same in principle. The principle of God's work is the same today as it was in the past.

God chose the Israelites to be His people, and He also chose men from among the Gentiles to be His people (Acts 15:14). The Bible says that we are fellow citizens and members of the household of God (Eph. 2:19). It also says that we are the true Jews (Rom. 2:29). Hence, the history of the Israelites is a pattern to us. In this book we will consider the way God deals with His people; in other words, the way God edifies His people. Putting it another way, this book will show the kind of experience we must acquire before we can become the people of God. We will discuss this subject through a consideration of the history of Abraham, Isaac, and Jacob because each of these three persons occupies a particular place in the Bible.

TWO

The Bible shows us that God's people had two beginnings. The first beginning was with Abraham because God's selection and calling began with Abraham. The other beginning was with the nation of Israel. God told the Israelites that they would be a people to Him among all the nations. They would be a kingdom of priests and a holy nation (Exo. 19:5-6). Hence, Abraham was a definite beginning for God's people, and the nation of Israel was also a definite beginning for God's people. In between these two beginnings, God gained three persons, Abraham, Isaac, and Jacob. First there was Abraham, then there was Isaac, then Jacob, and then the nation of Israel. From that point on, the nation of Israel became the people of God, and God had a people of His own. Hence, we can say that Abraham, Isaac, and Jacob are the foundations of the nation of Israel. Without Abraham, Isaac, and Jacob, there would not be the nation of Israel, and without Abraham, Isaac, and Jacob, there would not be a people of God. God's people became His people through the experience of Abraham, Isaac, and Jacob.

THREE

It is interesting to note that God said, "I am…the God of Abraham, the God of Isaac, and the God of Jacob" (Exo. 3:6). He said this in the Old Testament, and the Lord Jesus quoted it in the New Testament. "I am the God of Abraham and the God of Isaac and the God of Jacob" is quoted in the Gospels of Matthew, Mark, and Luke (Matt. 22:32; Mark 12:26; Luke 20:37). Furthermore, the Lord Jesus said that we would see "Abraham and Isaac and Jacob…in the kingdom of God" (Luke 13:28), and that "many will come from the east and the west and will recline at table with Abraham and Isaac and Jacob in the kingdom of the heavens" (Matt. 8:11). Here, He does not mention anyone else's names, only the names of Abraham, Isaac, and Jacob. This shows that Abraham, Isaac, and Jacob each occupy a special place in the Bible.

FOUR

Why do Abraham, Isaac, and Jacob occupy such a special place in the Bible? It is because God wants to select a group of people to come under His name and to make them His people. Beginning with Abraham, God began to gain a people. God had a spiritual beginning with Abraham, and He did something in Abraham for the purpose of showing us the necessary experience that God's people have to go through. All of God's people have to go through the same kind of experiences. He did something in Abraham first, giving him some particular experiences, and through him He conveyed these experiences to all of His people. The nation of Israel is founded upon Abraham, Isaac, and Jacob. Hence, God has worked not only in Abraham, but also in Isaac, giving him some particular experiences, and through him He conveyed these experiences to all of His people as well. Similarly, God did some work in Jacob, giving him some particular experiences, and through him He conveyed these experiences to all of His people. The dealings which these three received before God and the experiences they went through culminated in a people of God. Hence, the total experiences of Abraham, Isaac, and Jacob are the experiences that all of God's people should have. The attainments of these three should be the attainments of all the people of God. It is not enough to make us God's people if we merely have Abraham's experience. It is not enough to make us God's people if we merely have Isaac's experience, and it is not enough to make us God's people if we merely have Jacob's experience. We must have the attainments of Abraham plus Isaac plus Jacob before we can become God's people.

God told Isaac, "I am the God of Abraham thy father...I am with thee, and will bless thee, and multiply thy seed for my servant Abraham's sake" (Gen. 26:24). He told Jacob, "I am the Lord God of Abraham thy father, and the God of Isaac: the land whereon thou liest, to thee will I give it, and to thy seed" (28:13). He also told the Israelites, "I will bring you in unto the land, concerning the which I did swear to give it to Abraham, to Isaac, and to Jacob; and I will give it you for a heritage" (Exo. 6:8). This shows us that the Israelites entered into the inheritance of the three men, Abraham, Isaac, and Jacob. They did not have any inheritance of their own. Instead, they entered into the inheritance of the three men, Abraham, Isaac, and Jacob. Each of these men occupies a particular position before God. Their different spiritual experiences typify three different kinds of spiritual principles. In other words, all the people of God should have the element of

Abraham, the element of Isaac, and the element of Jacob in them. Without these elements, we cannot become God's people. God's people must have the element of Abraham, Isaac, and Jacob. All true Israelites and all genuine people of God must say that Abraham, Isaac, and Jacob are their ancestors. To say that Abraham is our ancestor is not enough, because Ishmael and his descendants can also say that their ancestor is Abraham. Neither is it enough to say that both Abraham and Isaac are our ancestors, because Esau and his descendants can say the same thing. God's people must say that their ancestors are Abraham, Isaac, and Jacob. Jacob must be included for complete qualification. All three must be together before we can justifiably be a people of God.

FIVE

Abraham's original name was Abram. Later God changed his name to Abraham (Gen. 17:5). Within both of these two names is the root *Abra,* which in the original language means "father." Abraham was a father himself, and the lesson he learned was to know God as the Father. Throughout his whole life, he learned this one lesson—knowing God as the Father.

What does it mean to know God as the Father? It means that everything is from God. The Lord Jesus said, "My Father is working until now, and I also am working" (John 5:17). He did not say, "My God is working until now," but "My Father is working until now." For God to be the Father means that God is the Creator, the unique Initiator. The Son was sent from the Father. "The Son can do nothing from Himself except what He sees the Father doing, for whatever that One does, these things the Son also does in like manner" (v. 19). This must be our experience. We must receive grace from God to realize that we cannot initiate anything. We are not worthy of initiating anything. Genesis 1 begins by saying, "In the beginning God...." In the beginning it was not us, but God. God is the Father, and everything originates from Him.

The day that God shows you that He is the Father will be a blessed day. On that day you will realize that you cannot do anything and that you are helpless. You will not have to try to hold yourself back from doing this thing or that thing.

Instead you will ask, "Has God initiated this?" This is the experience of Abraham. His experience shows us that he had no thought of becoming God's people. Abraham did not initiate anything. It was God who initiated. It was God who brought him from the other side of the Euphrates River (Gen. 12:1-5). God wanted him, and He called him out. Abraham never thought of this. Hallelujah! God wanted him and God did the work.

God is the Father. Abraham did not volunteer to go to the land flowing with milk and honey. God said it first, and then Abraham went and possessed it. He did not know anything about it beforehand. When he was called to go out, he did not know where he was going (Heb. 11:8). He left his father's land without knowing where he was going. This was Abraham. God was the Initiator of everything for him; he had nothing to do with it. If you know that God is the Father, you will not be so confident and will not say that you can do whatever you want. You will only say, "If the Lord is willing, I will do this and that. Whatever the Lord says, I will do." This does not mean that you should be indecisive. It means that you truly do not know what to do and that you only know after the Father has revealed His will.

This was not all. Abraham did not know that he was going to beget a son. He even had to receive his son from God. Abraham could not initiate anything. His son was given to him by God. This was Abraham.

Abraham knew God as the Father. This kind of knowledge is not a knowledge in doctrine. It is a knowledge in which one is brought to the point of confessing, "God, I am not the source. You are the source of everything, and You are my source. Without You, I cannot have a beginning." This was Abraham. If we do not have Abraham's realization, we cannot be God's people. The first lesson we have to learn is to realize that we can do nothing and that everything depends on God. He is the Father, and He is the Initiator of everything.

SIX

What is the lesson we learn from Isaac? Galatians 4 says that Isaac is the promised son (v. 23). In Isaac we see that everything comes from the Father. The history of Abraham, Isaac, and Jacob in Genesis 11 through 50 shows us that Isaac was an ordinary and unexceptional man. He was not like Abraham, and he was not like Jacob. Abraham came from the other side of the great river; he was a pioneer. Isaac was not like this. But neither was Isaac like Jacob, whose life was filled with difficulties and who suffered many dealings. Isaac's whole life was an enjoyment of his father's inheritance. It is true that Isaac dug a few wells. But even the wells were first dug by his father. "And Isaac digged again the wells of water, which they had digged in the days of Abraham his father; for the Philistines had stopped them after the death of Abraham: and he called their names after the names by which his father had called them" (Gen. 26:18). The lesson that Isaac teaches us is that we have nothing other than what we have inherited from the Father. Paul asked a question: "And what do you have that you did not receive?" (1 Cor. 4:7). In other words, there is nothing that we have that has not been received. All that we have comes from the Father. This is Isaac.

Many people cannot be in the position of Abraham because they cannot be in the position of Isaac. Many people fail to become Abraham because they fail to become Isaac. It is impossible to have the experience of Abraham without the experience of Isaac. It is also impossible to have the experience of Isaac without the experience of Abraham. We have to see that God is the Father and that everything proceeds from Him. We also have to see that we are sons and that everything we have is from Him. The life of the Son which we inherit comes from Him. In the eyes of God we are only those who receive. Salvation is received, victory is received, justification is received, sanctification is received, forgiveness is received, and freedom is received. The principle of receiving is the principle of Isaac. We have to say, Hallelujah! Hallelujah! Everything we have is from God. We see from God's Word that everything He promised to Abraham was promised also to Isaac. God did not give anything additional to Isaac; He gave Isaac what He gave his father. This is our salvation; this is our liberation.

SEVEN

Now let us come to Jacob. Many Christians see that God is the source of everything. They also see that everything they have comes through receiving. But there is a problem: Many Christians do not receive. We know that everything we have comes by receiving and that if we do not receive anything, we will be left with vanity and emptiness. But we still do not receive, and we still try to do things ourselves. Why? We do not overcome by the law of life; instead, we try to overcome by our own will. Why? One reason is that the principle of Jacob is still in us. The activity of the flesh is still present, the power of the soul is still present, and the natural life is still present. We know doctrinally that God is the Initiator of everything, yet in reality we initiate many things. We remember a doctrine for two weeks, but by the third week we have forgotten it. Then we try to initiate something again. We behave this way because Jacob is still present within us. If a doctrine of overcoming or a teaching of sanctification only tells us that everything comes from God and that everything is received, without telling us that the natural life needs to be dealt with, the doctrine of overcoming and the teaching of sanctification are incomplete and impractical. If a teaching does not touch the soul-life, it will only make us happy for a few days. Then everything will be over. We have to see that God is the Head of all things. We have to see that we are those who receive. At the same time, we have to see that our natural life must be checked. Only then will we see the goodness of the Son and the way of submission to the Father. Whether or not we can receive the promise of the Son and whether or not we can take the way of the Father depend on whether we accept the discipline of the Holy Spirit and whether we are willing to have our natural life touched. We can see this from the life of Jacob.

The outstanding characteristic of Jacob's natural constitution was his cleverness. He was an exceptionally clever person. He could deceive anyone. He deceived his brother, father, and uncle. He could devise anything, he could do everything, and he could achieve anything. He was not like his father, who was just a son. He went to his uncle empty-handed and came back with his hands full. This was Jacob.

What is the lesson we learn from Jacob? Abraham speaks to us of the Father, Isaac speaks to us of the Son, and Jacob speaks to us of the Holy Spirit. It does not mean that Jacob represents the Holy Spirit, but that his experiences represent the work of the Holy Spirit. Jacob's history is a type of the discipline of the Holy Spirit. We see a crafty person who was filled with schemes and deceits. But at the same time, we see a person whom the Holy Spirit disciplined step by step. He held his older brother's heel, yet he still ended up being the younger brother. He supplanted his brother with a pottage of lentils and usurped the birthright, but he, not his brother, eventually had to run away from home. He received his father's blessing, but he, not his brother, became a wanderer. When he went to stay with his uncle, he wanted to marry Rachel, but Laban gave him Leah, not Rachel first. For twenty years, the drought consumed him in the day, and the frost consumed him by night (Gen. 31:40). Indeed, he lived a toilsome and hard life. All these experiences were the discipline of the Holy Spirit; they were the trials that a clever man had to go through. Those who can scheme and who are resourceful will see God's hand upon them. The natural life has to be pressed out. Jacob's history is a picture of the discipline of the Holy Spirit.

Some brothers and sisters are exceptionally clever, thoughtful, shrewd, calculating, and resourceful. But we must remember that we do not walk in fleshly wisdom but in the grace of God (2 Cor. 1:12). Jacob experienced the continual discipline of the Holy Spirit. As a result, his cleverness was never able to have its way. On the night at Peniel, Jacob learned the greatest lesson; it was actually the best night of his life! He thought he could have his way with anyone and could similarly have his way with God. But when he came face to face with God, God touched the hollow of Jacob's thigh, and he became crippled (Gen. 32:25). The sinew of the hollow of the thigh is the strongest sinew in the whole body. For Jacob's hollow to be touched meant that God had touched the strongest part of his natural life. From that day on, he was

crippled! Before he was crippled, he was Jacob. After he
was crippled, Israel came into being (v. 28)! From that day on,
he was no longer a supplanter but one who was being supplanted. Before that time, he deceived his father. After that
day, he was deceived by his sons (37:28-35). The formerly
clever Jacob would never have been carried away by the
deception of his sons, because he was such a deceiver himself;
he would never have believed in others. The more a person
deceives, the more he does not trust in others, because he
judges others according to his own heart. But now things
were different. The latter Jacob was different from the former
Jacob. He no longer trusted in his own cleverness. This is why
he could be deceived by his own sons. He shed many tears,
and his natural strength was dealt with and was stripped
away by God. This is the kind of experience that makes us the
people of God. One day God will shine on you and show you
how evil, wicked, and conniving you are. When God shows
you who you are, you will not be able to lift up your head.
God's light will terminate you and force you to admit that you
are finished. You will acknowledge that you dare not serve
God anymore and that you are not qualified to serve Him any
longer! From that point on, you will no longer trust in yourself. This is the discipline of the Holy Spirit.

EIGHT

In conclusion, Abraham shows us that everything is of
God; we cannot do anything by ourselves. Isaac shows us that
everything comes from God, and our place is to receive. But if
we only receive and do not have the discipline of the Holy
Spirit, something will go wrong. This is what Jacob shows us.
One day the Lord will come to us, touch us, and twist the
hollow of our thigh; He will deal with our natural life. Then
we will become humble and follow the Lord in fear and trembling. Then we will not be careless and make proposals
rashly. How easy it is for us to make proposals, and how easy
it is for us to act without prayer. How easy it is for us to
develop a confidence apart from God. God has to touch our
natural life in a drastic way; He has to break apart our natural life and show us that we can do nothing by ourselves.

From that day on, we will be lame men. Being lame does not mean that we cannot walk; rather, it means that every time we walk, we realize our weakness and our lameness. This is the common trait of all those who know God. Before God brings a man to such a point, he does not have the experience of Peniel. All those who are still resourceful, confident, and powerful have not experienced the discipline of the Holy Spirit.

May God open our eyes to see the relationship between these three kinds of experiences. All three experiences are particular experiences, and yet all three are interrelated in their accomplishment. We cannot have just one or two of the three. We have to be clear about all three experiences before we can advance in the way of God.

CHAPTER TWO

THE CALLING OF ABRAHAM

Scripture Reading: Heb. 11:8-10; Acts 7:2-5; Gal. 3:8; Gen. 11:31—12:3, 7a; 13:14-17; 14:21-23

We have mentioned previously that God desires to gain a group of men who are called by His name and who are His people. He wants to gain a group of people who can say that they belong to God and that they are God's people. In order to achieve this goal, He first worked on Abraham, then on Isaac, and finally on Jacob. The experiences of Abraham plus Isaac plus Jacob are the basic experiences of all who desire to be God's people. This means that being God's people is not just a haphazard thing. In order to be God's people, we must have some definite experiences in Him. We have to pass through certain dealings and certain trainings before we can become God's people and before we can truly live for God on this earth. The basic experiences for being God's people are the experiences of Abraham, the experiences of Isaac, and the experiences of Jacob. In other words, although many people can be called by God's name and outwardly be known as God's people, they are not qualified to become God's people unless they see that everything they have is from God, that everything is received, and that everything of the natural life has to be laid aside by God. If they are not such persons, they cannot be of much use in God's hand.

ABRAHAM BEING THE BEGINNING
OF THE RECOVERY WORK OF GOD

Let us come to the story of Abraham. All those who read the Bible will not fail to realize the importance of Abraham. His name is mentioned at the beginning of the New Testament. The Lord Jesus spoke of Abraham many times in His discourses; He did not mention Adam. He said, "Before Abraham came into being, I am" (John 8:58). He did not say, "Before Adam came into being, I am." He did not say to the Jews, "Your father Adam," but "Your father Abraham" (v. 56). He took Abraham as the starting point.

May the Lord open our eyes to see that Abraham is the starting point in God's plan of redemption and in His work of recovery. Romans 4 tells us that Abraham is the father of all those who believe (v. 17). Every believer has his beginning in Abraham. The starting point is Abraham, not Adam. Adam is the beginning of sin; sin entered the world through one man (5:12). That beginning was a corrupted beginning. Even though Abel offered sacrifices to God by faith, he was only a good person individually; we cannot receive blessing from him; hence, he is not the beginning of the recovery work of God. Even though Enoch walked with God, he was also only a good individual; we cannot receive blessing from him; hence, he cannot be the beginning of the recovery work of God either. Noah feared God, and his household entered the ark, but again he was only a good person individually; we cannot receive blessing from him; hence, he cannot be the beginning of the recovery work of God either. All of these three persons were good, but they were only good individually. Abel, Enoch, Noah, and Abraham believed in God. But there is a difference between Abraham and Abel, Enoch, and Noah. Abraham occupies a much more important place in God's plan of redemption than do Abel, Enoch, and Noah because God's recovery work began with him.

We must see that Abraham is different from all the other men. From the time that Adam sinned, there has been a line of sin. Although Abel was a good man, he could not deal with the line of sin; although Enoch was a good man, he could not deal with the tide of sin either; and although Noah was a good man, he could not change the sinful situation. Man had become fallen and had failed. Although these three men were good, they were good men as individuals only; they could not change the sinful situation. There is a great difference between being good individually and turning a situation around. The first time God used a man to turn the sinful situation was when He used Abraham. Before Abraham, God did some work in individuals, but He did not do anything to recover the sinful situation. The first time God moved His hand to turn the sinful situation was in His selection of Abraham. In other words, the first point of recovery was with Abraham. The tide of sin had been going on, and Abel, Enoch, and Noah were just three good rocks in the midst of this sinful torrent. Abraham was the first person through whom God turned the tide. God raised up Abraham and through him brought in the work of deliverance. Through him the Savior came and redemption came. This is why the gospel in the New Testament begins with Abraham. May the Lord be merciful to us that we do not engage ourselves merely in the exposition of the Bible or in helping others to understand some Bible knowledge. We look to God's mercy to show us what God is doing.

Redemption was accomplished by the Lord Jesus, yet its beginning was with Abraham. God's recovery work has been continuing throughout the ages until today. It will continue until the time of the millennium. However, the starting point was with Abraham. In other words, the center of redemption is the Lord Jesus, and the consummation of redemption will be at the end of the millennium at the commencement of the new heaven and new earth. However, the beginning of redemption was with Abraham. From the time of Abraham until the end of the millennium, God has been doing a work of recovery continually. During the long process of this work of recovery, the Lord Jesus Christ is the center, but we should never forget that the starting point was Abraham.

This is what is special about Abraham. God's selection of Abraham was very different from His gracious dealings with Abel, Enoch, and Noah. When God gained Abel, He only gained Abel. When God gained Enoch, He only gained Enoch. When God gained Noah, He only gained Noah. But when God chose Abraham, He did not gain just Abraham. When Abraham was called, God told him clearly why he was called. God told him to leave his country, his kindred, and his father's house and to go into the land of Canaan; He promised to make him a great nation in whom all the families of the earth

would be blessed (Gen. 12:1-3). In other words, the calling
and choosing of Abraham was for the purpose of recovering a
sinful situation; it was not for Abraham alone as an individual. Abraham was called because God wanted to use him. He
was called to be a vessel and called for a work. He was not
called simply to receive grace. It is one thing for a person to
be called to receive grace. It is another thing for a person to
be called to transmit grace. Abraham's calling was not just
for him to receive grace, but for him to be a transmitter of
grace.

GOD'S PURPOSE IN CALLING ABRAHAM

God's purpose in calling Abraham was to recover man
from the sinful situation. We should not consider the choosing
of Abraham to be a personal matter. Abraham's being chosen
by God was for the purpose of recovering man from his sinful
situation. We should carefully consider the items included in
the calling of Abraham and the kind of things brought about
through such a calling. In Abraham's calling we see God's
purpose, plan, and predestination. We also see the solution to
the problems of sin and the devil. May the Lord open our eyes
to see these things.

Genesis 12:1 says, "Now the Lord had said unto Abram,
Get thee out of thy country, and from thy kindred, and from
thy father's house, unto a land that I will show thee." God
called Abraham with the purpose that he would get out of his
country, and from his kindred, and from his father's house.
This is a matter of inheritance. Verse 2 says, "And I will make
of thee a great nation, and I will bless thee, and make thy
name great; and thou shalt be a blessing." "A great nation"
speaks of a people. Verse 3 says, "And I will bless them that
bless thee, and curse him that curseth thee: and in thee shall
all families of the earth be blessed." "In thee shall all families
of the earth be blessed"—this is the ultimate goal of God's
selection of Abraham. In God's selection of Abraham, three
things were included: (1) bringing him into the land which
God would show him, (2) making him a great nation that
would become God's people, and (3) blessing all the families of
the earth through him.

"Unto a Land That I Will Show Thee"

God called Abraham to leave his country, his kindred, and his father's house and go to a land that He would show him. Abraham came from Ur of Chaldea, a land which served idols. His father Terah dwelt there and served the idols (Josh. 24:2). God called Abraham out of this land. On the negative side, it was for the purpose of taking him out of his country, his kindred, and his father's house and forsaking the service of the idols. On the positive side, it was for the purpose of bringing him into the land that God would show him, the land of Canaan, and serving the most high God, possessor of heaven and earth.

God called Abraham so that he would go into Canaan, live there, express God, and carry out the authority of the heavens. God intended to give the land to his descendants. Through him and his descendants, God intended to claim the land for Himself and to carry out His authority and express His glory in the land. This was God's first reason for calling Abraham.

In Matthew 6 the Lord Jesus taught the disciples to pray, saying, "Our Father who is in the heavens, Your name be sanctified; Your kingdom come; Your will be done, as in heaven, so also on earth" (vv. 9-10). God's intention is for His people to bring His authority and His will to earth. Today the church should be the place where God's glory is expressed and the place where His authority and will are carried out. Wherever God's people obey His will and allow His authority to spread among them, that is the place where God's authority and God's will are executed. God wants to gain a group of men on earth to be His people. This means that God wants to gain a way among men so that His authority and His will can be done on earth as they are done in heaven. This was God's goal in calling Abraham. It is also His goal in calling us to be His people.

"I Will Make of Thee a Great Nation"

God called Abraham not only for the purpose of bringing him to the land that He would show him but also for the purpose of making a great nation out of him. God's goal is to gain a group of men to be His people. God called Abraham with the purpose of making him and his descendants His people. In other words, God's choosing of His people began with Abraham. He called one man out from among so many men. Thereafter, God revealed Himself to this man, and His salvation was to be accomplished through this man. Salvation would come out of this one man. God would reach His goal through the man He chose and called.

Abraham was selected. This means that God called out for Himself one man from among many men. God wants to gain a group of people for Himself. In the Old Testament there was a nation, Israel, because God wanted a people on this earth, that is, He wanted a group of people who were separated unto God, who were for His glory, and who belonged to Him.

Although God let the Israelites go in regard to many of the sins that they committed, He would not let them go when they committed the sin of idolatry. For God's people to worship idols is a very serious sin. God's place can never be usurped by idols. God's purpose in choosing a people is for them to become His testimony on the earth. What should they testify? They should testify God. God has placed Himself in the midst of His people. In other words God's people are the vessel which contains God. Wherever there are God's people, there is God's testimony. Rabshakeh, a general of the king of Assyria, the enemy of the children of Israel, said, "Where are the gods of Hamath, and of Arpad? where are the gods of Sepharvaim, Hena, and Ivah?...Who are they among all the gods of the countries, that have delivered their country out of mine hand, that the Lord should deliver Jerusalem out of mine hand?" (2 Kings 18:34-35). This shows us that before the enemies of the Israelites could deal with the Israelites, they had to first deal with Jehovah because the Israelites were one with Jehovah. God has placed Himself in the midst of His people. He has placed Himself, His glory, His authority, and His power in the midst of His people.

Acts 15:14 says, "God...visited the Gentiles to take out from them a people for His name." This is a picture of the New Testament. In the New Testament the church constitutes

God's people. All of God's testimony, work, and will are found in the church today.

God's goal is to gain a group of people unto Himself. His goal is to gain a group of people who will declare, "I belong to Jehovah. I am the Lord's." This is why the Bible pays so much attention to a person's confession of Christ. The Lord said, "Everyone who confesses in Me before men, the Son of Man will also confess in him before the angels of God; but he who denies Me before men will be denied before the angels of God" (Luke 12:8-9). The Lord wants to gain men who will confess His name. Many times, confessing Christ is not just preaching the gospel, but declaring, "I belong to the Lord. I belong to God!" This is God's testimony. In this way God will gain something. God wants to gain a group of people, who will confess, "I belong to God, and I am for Him."

"In Thee Shall All
Families of the Earth Be Blessed"

God also said to Abraham, "In thee shall all families of the earth be blessed" (Gen. 12:3). This shows that God has not forgotten the nations. God does not bless the nations of the earth directly. Rather, He blesses them through Abraham. God chose one man, and this one man became a vessel. From this man there was a family, and from that family a nation, and from that nation all the families of the earth are blessed. God does not bless the nations directly. Rather, He worked on one man first, and through this one man all the nations of the earth are blessed. God fully deposited His grace, power, and authority into this one man, and then through this one man dispensed all these things to all men. This is the principle of Abraham's selection. This principle continues until today. Hence, the most important issue for God is the choosing of His vessel. Indeed, those who are chosen as vessels should know Him! Whether or not the families of the earth would be blessed depended fully on Abraham. In other words, God's eternal purpose and His plan are joined to the men He has chosen. The standing or failure of God's chosen men determines the success or failure of God's purpose and plan.

This is why Abraham had to go through so many experiences and had to receive so much from God before he could dispense what he had received to others. It is no wonder that Abraham had to go through so many trials and encounter so many problems. This was the only way that others could receive help and benefit from him. Abraham knew God; therefore, he is the father of those who believe. Those who are of faith are the sons of Abraham (Gal. 3:7); they are begotten of Abraham. We know that all spiritual works are based on the principle of *begetting,* not on the principle of *preaching.* Sons are begotten; they do not come about through preaching. God's way of recovery requires man to believe. Only those who believe will be justified. What did God do? First He brought one man to the point of believing so that he would be a believer; from this believer many more believers were begotten.

We have to remember that it is useless to preach without begetting. That kind of preaching will only make men understand doctrines, and the doctrines will pass from one mouth to another. After they circle the earth and come back to the speaker, they will still be nothing more than doctrines. What good will it do for a man to zealously preach the doctrine of salvation if he himself does not know God and is not begotten of God? But if a man is not merely preaching the doctrine of salvation with his mouth, but is testifying of his salvation and how he has met God, others will touch something real. Only this kind of person will beget others. God's principle of work is to do something in one person first and then beget others through him. God's work is living, and when He sows the living seed into a person, the seed will grow. Paul told the Corinthians, "It is not to shame you that I write these things but to admonish you as my beloved children....for in Christ Jesus I have begotten you through the gospel" (1 Cor. 4:14-15). Begetting is a great principle in spiritual work. The principle of spiritual work is one of begetting, not of preaching.

May God open our eyes to see the vanity of preaching. It is useless to preach something to others without having that thing ourselves. If we have the seed, we have the growth. Without the seed there cannot be growth. God's work is related to life; it is not an empty doctrine. Once you pass through a certain pathway ordained by God, you will have the ability to beget. Otherwise, nothing will avail. In order to bless all the families of the earth, God first had to work on Abraham. In order to have a group of believers, God first had to gain one believer. Abraham was the first one who believed. Then many more believers were begotten through him. All the families of the earth are blessed not through a sermon they hear, but through a life they receive. God worked on Abraham first, and then through him expanded His work to many people. One day when the city which Abraham eagerly waited for descends, the city whose Architect and Builder is God (Heb. 11:10), all the families of the earth will be fully blessed, and God's eternal plan will be fully consummáted. God's work of redemption began at the time of Abraham. God worked in Abraham in order to make him a vessel, and this was not for Abraham alone. Through Abraham God reached others.

GOD'S TWO CALLINGS OF ABRAHAM

Now we will consider how Abraham was called to follow God. In reading Joshua 24, we find that Abraham was born into a family that served idols. Therefore, it is interesting to note that God's work of recovery began from Abraham. God purposely chose such a person. This shows us that "it is not of him who wills, nor of him who runs, but of God who shows mercy" (Rom. 9:16). Abraham could never have thought that God would call him. He had nothing to boast of in himself. He was an ordinary man who was no different from anyone else. It was not Abraham who made himself different from others; it was God who made him different. God called him and made him different. Hence, we have to know God's sovereignty. If God wants to do something, He will do it. Abraham was the same as anyone else. There was no reason for God to choose him, yet God chose him. The first lesson Abraham had to learn was to know that God is the One who initiates everything. God called Abraham twice. Let us consider how God called Abraham the first time, and how he answered God's calling.

The First Calling in Ur

The first calling was in Mesopotamia, in Ur of Chaldea. Stephen said, "The God of glory appeared to our father Abraham while he was in Mesopotamia, before he dwelt in Haran" (Acts 7:2). From this we see that God called Abraham before he left Ur. The very God of glory appeared to Abraham and called him out of his country, his kindred, and his father's house, unto the land that God would show him. Did Abraham believe? Hebrews 11 tells us that Abraham believed. Indeed, once a man sees God's glory, there is no way for him not to believe. Abraham was an ordinary man, the same as we. He believed because the God of glory appeared to him. God was the reason and the cause of him becoming a believer. It was God who initiated, and it was God who caused him to believe.

Was Abraham's faith great from the beginning? No. What did he do after he heard God's call? "And Terah took Abram his son, and Lot the son of Haran his son's son, and Sarai his daughter-in-law, his son Abram's wife; and they went forth with them from Ur of the Chaldees, to go into the land of Canaan; and they came unto Haran, and dwelt there" (Gen. 11:31). Acts 7:2 says that Abraham heard the call in Mesopotamia. Hebrews 11:8 says that Abraham had also believed. The incident in Genesis 11:31 came after the one in Acts 7:2 and Hebrews 11:8. We should take note of the word here: "And Terah took Abram his son, and Lot the son of Haran his son's son, and Sarai his daughter-in-law, his son Abram's wife; and they went forth with them from Ur of the Chaldees." This was the first expression of Abraham's faith. He was not much better than we. God told him to leave his country. Did he leave? Yes, he left, but God said that he should also leave his kindred. Did he do this? He only did half of it; Lot still followed him. God said that he should leave his father's house, but he took his father's house with him. Abraham's leaving was not his own decision, but the decision of his father—"And *Terah took* Abram his son." We do not know why Terah was willing to go. Perhaps Abraham told his father, "God called me. I have to go." Perhaps Terah went along because of his love for his son. We cannot say with certainty that this was the case. But we can say that the one who did not receive the calling became the initiating party, while the one who received the calling became the follower! Perhaps some would say, "Isn't it better that the whole household was saved?" We admit that it was a good thing for the whole household to be saved. However, Abraham's calling was not a matter of salvation but a matter of ministry. The calling of Noah to enter the ark was a matter of salvation, but the calling of Abraham to enter Canaan was a matter of ministry. It was a matter of the accomplishment of God's plan. This is the difference between Abraham and Noah. It was right for Noah to bring his whole family into the ark, but it was wrong for Abraham to bring his father's house into Canaan. If there are some in our household who are not saved, it is right to bring them to salvation. But if God has called us to be His minister and His vessel, we cannot bring along those who do not have the calling.

Abraham's beginning was very ordinary. He was called, and he believed. But he did not believe in an exceptional way; he merely believed. He wanted to go along, but he did not fully oblige. He wanted to obey, and he felt uneasy not obeying. He wanted to leave, but he did not leave in a clear way. He was not much different from us. Therefore, none of us should be discouraged, and no one should think that he is through or hopeless. We have to know that our hope rests in God.

What happened after Abraham followed his father and left? They stopped halfway. God wanted him to go to Canaan, but he stopped in Haran and dwelt there. He did not realize that God had to do a thorough work in him before he could become His vessel. He was not clear about God's commission and ministry for him. He still did not understand why he had to pay such a great price. This is also true of us. Because we do not know God's mind, we ask, "Why does God treat me this way? Why doesn't He treat me like He treated Noah? Noah could be together with his whole family, yet I have to leave my father's house!" We have to remember that a cheap vessel comes with a cheap price, while an expensive vessel comes with an expensive price. God wanted Abraham to be a vessel of honor, so His demands on him were greater than on others. We must never misunderstand God's way in dealing with us. We do not know how God will use us. All of our experiences are for our future service. We should never say, "Others can do this and that. Why can't I do the same?" We have to remember that God trains every person in a special way because He wants to use that person in a special way. Our special usefulness comes from our special training. Therefore, we should not be discontent or disobedient. It is most foolish to resist God's hand or to ask why God does this and that.

God's work on Abraham shows His intention with Abraham, yet Abraham did not understand. He did not know why God wanted him to leave his country, his kindred, and his father's house. He only went a short distance from his country. He wanted to leave his kindred, but still brought Lot with him. He wanted to leave his father's house, but it was too difficult for him, and he ended up taking it along with him. He did not see his ministry and did not know what God was doing. As a result, his days in Haran were wasted days, delayed days, and useless days.

Later his father died. But he was still unwilling to give up his nephew; he brought Lot with him. Terah was only a hindrance to Abraham while he was alive, but Lot became a burden to God's people even after his death. Because of Lot's actions, two sons were produced. One was Moab, the father of the Moabites; the other was Ben-ammi, the father of the Ammonites. Both the Moabites and the Ammonites eventually became problems to the Israelites.

The Second Calling in Haran

In Genesis 12, God called Abraham the second time. The first time was in Ur, while the second time was in Haran. God said, "Get thee out of thy country, and from thy kindred, and from thy father's house, unto a land that I will show thee: and I will make of thee a great nation,...and in thee shall all families of the earth be blessed" (vv. 1-3). This was the same calling as the original calling. He heard this calling once again in Haran. The first calling only brought him halfway. The second calling brought him all the way into Canaan. We have to thank the Lord unceasingly because He never gives up! God's persistence is most precious! We become Christians because of God's persistence, not because of our holding on to God. If it were up to us, we would have let go long ago. Abraham was able to reach Canaan because God was persistent. We can be Christians because God holds us fast. Thank the Lord that He is a God who will not let go.

In appearing to and calling Abraham, we see that God is a God who is never defeated. God is the God of glory! From the fall of Adam until the time of God's appearance to Abraham, the Bible records many of God's speakings to man, but it does not say that God appeared to man. The first time that the Bible records God's appearance to man was in Mesopotamia when He appeared to Abraham. This is why we say that God's work of recovery began with Abraham. Prior to this, God never appeared to man. But on this occasion, God appeared to Abraham. Although two thousand years of human history had elapsed since the fall, and although humanly speaking, God had apparently failed, His appearance tells us that He really had not failed. His goal was not lost, because the God of glory appeared to Abraham! God is the God of glory! He is the Alpha and the Omega. He is still the God of glory! Nothing can be more sure than the God of glory, and nothing can last longer than His glory. From Adam to Abraham, two thousand years passed, not twenty years or two hundred years. Although God did not appear to man for a long time, He had not failed, for He was the God of glory.

The God of glory appeared to Abraham and told him what he should do. Abraham not only received God's appearance but was entrusted with God's will. He knew what God wanted him to do. God told him, "Get thee...unto a land that I will show thee: and I will make of thee a great nation,...and in thee shall all families of the earth be blessed." God said this to show Abraham that in spite of two thousand years of man's failure and in spite of the multiplicity of man's sin, God was coming in now to recover him. God was bringing in a recovery work through Abraham.

Abraham heard and believed in God's first calling, and he left Ur of Chaldea. But he followed his father to stay in

Haran; he only went halfway. It is hard for us to forget our salvation story, but it is easy for us to forget the vision of our calling to the ministry. It is easy for us to drop our calling. The minute we become slightly busy with our service to God, we easily forget our ministry and God's purpose. Abraham forgot God's calling of him. Therefore, he needed God to speak to him again, and God spoke the same thing to him in Haran. Thank the Lord that He speaks to us again and again to ensure that we know what He wants to do.

Abraham heard the calling. The faith that was invoked in him the first time when he was called came back. His faith was recovered, and he was able to journey onward again.

CHAPTER THREE

ABRAHAM AND THE LAND OF CANAAN

Scripture Reading: Acts 7:2; Gen. 12:4—13:18; 14:11-23

Abraham's history can be divided into three sections. Genesis 12 through 14 form the first section. The emphasis in this section is the land of Canaan. Chapters fifteen through twenty-two form the second section. The emphasis in this section is his son. Chapters twenty-three to twenty-five form the third section. It covers the events which happened in Abraham's old age. Let us first come to the first section.

Genesis 12:4-5 says, "So Abram departed, as the Lord had spoken unto him; and Lot went with him: and Abram was seventy and five years old when he departed out of Haran. And Abram took Sarai his wife, and Lot his brother's son, and all their substance that they had gathered, and the souls that they had gotten in Haran; and they went forth to go into the land of Canaan; and into the land of Canaan they came." After Abraham heard God's second calling in Haran, he left Haran and came to Canaan. But we have to realize that it is possible for a person to reach Canaan without knowing why he is there. Do not think that once we see the vision, everything will follow. It is one thing to see the heavenly vision, but it is another thing to not disobey the heavenly vision. After Abraham arrived in Canaan, verse 7 says, "And the Lord appeared unto Abram, and said, Unto thy seed will I give this land: and there builded he an altar unto the Lord, who appeared unto him." This is the second time God appeared to Abraham and the third time He spoke to him. God appeared and spoke once more so that Abraham would have a clear and fresh impression of the things God had committed to him.

It is easy for us to lose the vision of God's calling. Even if we are consciously trying to be a proper Christian, it is still possible for us to lose our vision. We can lose our vision even while we are working diligently day after day. Do not think that only mundane things can blur our vision; even spiritual things can blur our vision. If we do not live continuously in God's appearing, it will be easy for us to lose the vision of our calling. The calling that the church has received is the same as the calling that Abraham received. But many people have not seen the hope of this calling. Therefore, Paul prayed, "That you may know what is the hope of His calling" (Eph. 1:18). "Hope" indicates the content of this calling, the things included in God's calling. May God deliver us from selfish thoughts. We know that God calls us with a definite goal. Our salvation is to fulfill this goal. If we have not seen the substance of Abraham's calling, we will not see the meaning of our own calling. If we have not seen the key to Abraham's calling, we will not see our own ministry. If we do not see this, we will be like those who build a house without a foundation. How easy it is for us to forget what God wants to do! Many times, when we have too much to do and the work becomes a little more hectic, we lose sight of our spiritual calling. We need to come again and again to the Lord and beseech Him: "Appear to me again and again, and speak to me again and again!" We need to have a continuous seeing, an eternal seeing; we need to see God's goal and what God is doing.

Abraham had reached Canaan. After he arrived in Canaan, several things happened. First, he built three altars in Canaan. Second, he was tested three times in Canaan.

ABRAHAM BUILDING AN ALTAR

After Abraham arrived in Canaan, the Bible tells us that the first place he went to was Sichem (or Shechem). In Shechem he built an altar. The second place he went to was Bethel, and there he also built an altar. Later he left Bethel and went to Egypt. Then he went from Egypt to the south, and from the south he went back to Bethel, staying in between Bethel and Hai (or Ai), the place where he first built an altar. Later he went to another place, Hebron, and built another altar. In these three places, Abraham built three altars. All three places have an altar, and all three places are sanctified. The Bible shows us that God used these three places—Shechem, Bethel, and Hebron—to represent Canaan. In God's eyes, Canaan carries the characteristics of Shechem, Bethel, and Hebron. The characteristics of these places are the characteristics of Canaan. Once we see these three places, we will see what Canaan is like. Let us consider the characteristics of these three places.

Shechem (Shoulder)—the Place of Strength

"And Abram passed through the land unto the place of Sichem, unto the plain of Moreh....And the Lord appeared unto Abram, and said, Unto thy seed will I give this land: and there builded he an altar unto the Lord, who appeared unto him" (Gen. 12:6-7). Abraham arrived in Shechem. The meaning of the word *Shechem* in the original language is "shoulder." In the human body the shoulder is the place with the most strength. The shoulder can lift what the hand cannot pick up. Therefore *Shechem* can also mean "strength." The first characteristic of Canaan is strength. This means that God's strength is in Canaan. Canaan is not just a place flowing with milk and honey; it is also a place of strength.

The Bible shows us that God's power is not only a miraculous power, but the power of life; it is a power which satisfies man. The Lord said, "Whoever drinks of the water that I will give him shall by no means thirst forever; but the water that I will give him will become in him a spring of water gushing up into eternal life" (John 4:14). How powerful this is! This is the power of life! The Lord's life has a power that satisfies! Once a man possesses the Lord's life, he will never thirst again, because he will be inwardly satisfied. Those who are inwardly satisfied and who have received life within are the most powerful ones. They are Shechem, the shoulder, and are powerful to bear much burden. Thank and praise the Lord that one characteristic of Canaan is the power of life.

In Shechem there was the oak of Moreh (Gen. 12:6, ASV). The name *Moreh* means "teacher" or "teaching" in the original language. It has something to do with knowledge. The oak of Moreh was in Shechem. This means that knowledge comes from power and that knowledge is the result of power. In other words, genuine spiritual knowledge comes from the power of Christ. If we do not have the satisfying power of the life of Christ, we will not have genuine spiritual knowledge and will not be able to convey anything spiritual to others. If God is to have a vessel to recover His testimony on earth, such a vessel must be a particular vessel. With such a vessel, the first need is not to be taught doctrines; the first need is to be satisfied and to acquire the power of life. Then there will be real knowledge. There is a tremendous difference here. One is a matter of doctrine, while the other is a matter of life. One is the result of hearing something outward, and the other is seeing something inward. One results in forgetting what one hears, and the other results in receiving something unforgettable. If anyone says, "I no longer remember the cross, because no one has preached about the cross during the past few months," this proves that the cross he has is only in doctrine and memory; it is not in life. We have to remember that all genuine knowledge is found in the power of life. Christ's power is our power. Because we have something within us, we can share the same thing with others. The Lord gives us inward power and inward knowledge. *Moreh* comes from power.

We have to be careful not to give to others just the doctrines that we have heard. We must have the spiritual thing itself before we can give it to others. In spiritual matters the clever ones end up taking the circuitous way. They trust too much in their cleverness, and as a result they wander farther away from the spiritual path. May the Lord deliver us from objective teachings.

Bethel (the House of God)—the Body of Christ

"And he removed from thence unto a mountain on the east of Bethel, and pitched his tent, having Bethel on the west, and Hai on the east: and there he builded an altar unto the Lord, and called upon the name of the Lord" (Gen. 12:8). God brought Abraham not only to Shechem, but to Bethel as well. The name *Bethel* in the original language means "the house of God." God is not after hundreds and thousands of strong, but uncoordinated, men like Samson, and He is not after a pile of unorganized, living stones. God's intention is to build a temple—the house of God. One characteristic of Canaan is that God's people are the temple of God and the house of God. Hebrews 3:6 tells us that it was not Moses who was over this house, but the Son of God who is over this house.

God wants to raise up a vessel to fulfill His purpose. Such a vessel must be His house. A few particularly gifted gospel preachers will not fulfill such a purpose, nor will a few capable revivalists do the job. It is not enough to have Shechem (power) only. There must also be Bethel. All the powerful ones must become God's house and the Body of Christ before they can become useful. God has to deliver us from all forms of individualism. God has not saved us only to be proper Christians, but to be God's house and one Body together with all His children. Therefore, we should not have our personal "liberty." Unfortunately, many Christians love their personal liberty and are very good at preserving their personal liberty! Brothers and sisters, if we are truly clear about the testimony of God's house, and if we know that God's vessel is a house, not individual, scattered stones, we will learn to submit to one another, reject any individual move, and take the same way as all of God's children.

God's house is not only a principle, but a life. The problem is that many Christians consider the Body of Christ merely as a principle; they have not seen the life of the Body of Christ. What good is it if we try to do something according to a principle without having the life to do it? We think that we should cooperate with one another in everything, and we often reluctantly agree to cooperate, but our heart has no taste for it. What is the use of doing such a thing? We have to remember that the Body is a life and not merely a principle. If we do not know that the Body is a life, and if we merely act according to a principle, we are only imitating in an outward way. Many Christians have never been dealt with by the Lord. They have heard that they should not act independently and that they should cooperate with others, and they try to practice cooperation. However, they do not realize that this is something that one cannot learn to do. Just as our relationship with Christ is not something we acquire by learning, our relationship with the Body of Christ is not something that we acquire by learning.

How can we know the life of the Body? The basic condition for knowing the life of the Body is that our tent must be pitched between Bethel and Ai. To our west there should be Bethel, and to our east there should be Ai. It is not merely a matter of Bethel, but a matter of Ai as well. The name *Ai* means "a heap" in the original language. Bethel is a house, the house of God, while Ai is a heap, a desolate heap. The desolate heap signifies the old creation; Ai symbolizes the old creation. If we are to turn our face towards God's house, we must turn our back towards the desolate heap. In other words, unless a Christian is dealt with in his fleshly life, he cannot possibly know the Body of Christ. Only when we have Ai on the east will we have Bethel on the west. If we do not have Ai on our east, we will not have Bethel on our west. One begins his experience of the Body of Christ and enjoys and lives out the Body life by dealing with the life of the flesh. If we want to find out what the house of God is, we must deny the desolate heap on the negative side. Only after our natural life has been dealt with by God, and only after we have been subdued to realize that the natural life should be judged rather than praised, will we be joined spontaneously to the other brothers and sisters. Only then will we be able to live out the life of the Body of Christ. The only reason we cannot be joined to the other brothers and sisters is that the life of our old creation is too strong. Once the old creation within us is dealt with, we will spontaneously live out the life of the Body of Christ; we will see that we are a part of the Body of Christ and that we are in the Body. Hence, the life of the old creation must be dealt with and thoroughly denied. No matter what is in the heap, it is a desolate heap and not the house of God.

For those Christians who have not passed through the judgment of the old creation, the old creation is a boast to them. They still think that what they have in themselves is good. Although they admit with their mouth that they are weak and corrupt, they have never been judged in reality. They do not consider corruption to be corruption. Instead they consider corruption to be something lovable. They consider the part in them which cannot get along with others to be something noble. Whenever we find ourselves in this state, that is the time we need God's mercy the most.

One day God will bring us to the point where we realize our uselessness. We will lose our self-confidence. Only then will we come into God's house spontaneously. It is impossible to live the Body life without having the flesh dealt with. We must ask the Lord to show us that the Body of Christ is not just a principle, but a life.

Hebron (Fellowship)—the Principle of Fellowship

"Then Abram removed his tent, and came and dwelt in the plain of Mamre, which is in Hebron, and built there an altar unto the Lord" (Gen. 13:18).

The name *Hebron* means "fellowship" in the original language. God's house is a matter of life, while fellowship is a matter of living. It is impossible for one to live in Hebron without first passing through Bethel. We have to remember that Hebron comes after Bethel. Where there is God's house, there is fellowship. Fellowship is not a community organized by a number of people. Fellowship can only be found in the house of God. Without God's house it is impossible to have fellowship. If our natural life is not dealt with, we cannot have any fellowship. We live in the Body and have fellowship only when the natural life is dealt with.

Bethel appears to be the center of Canaan. God brought Abraham to Bethel to dwell there. As soon as Abraham left Bethel, he failed. When he came back from Egypt, God brought him back to Bethel, the place where he had built an altar. Only after he settled down in Bethel did God gradually move him to Hebron. This is very meaningful. One will be led into the fellowship only after he sees the house of God—the life of the Body of Christ.

The Body is a fact; it is a real, definite fact. In this Body we spontaneously communicate and fellowship with other children of the Lord. Once we turn our back towards Ai and judge the natural life, we will enter into the life of the Body of Christ and be brought into the fellowship spontaneously. Those who truly know the Body of Christ are freed from individualism spontaneously. They do not trust in themselves, and they realize that they are very weak. They fellowship with all the children of God. God must bring us to the point where we cannot go on without fellowship. God will show us that what is impossible with individuals is possible when it is done in fellowship. This is the meaning of Hebron.

In Shechem there was an oak called the oak of Moreh. In Hebron there were also oaks called the oaks of Mamre (Gen. 13:18, ASV). The name *Mamre* means "fatness" or "strength" in the original language. The result of fellowship is fatness and strength. All fatness, riches, and strength come from fellowship.

In summary, Shechem, Bethel, and Hebron signify the characteristics of Canaan. Although no one on the whole earth knows God, His people in Canaan know His power, His Body, and fellowship. As a result of seeing this, God's people become His testimony. They must maintain themselves in such a condition before they can bear God's testimony. Only when they bear these three characteristics will they be able to offer up burnt offerings, and only then will God accept the sacrifice. A sacrifice is not only an offering, but there is also the element of God's acceptance. We may want to offer many things to God which He absolutely does not want. All three places have altars. This means that these are the places that God wants and that God accepts.

If a Christian wants to maintain God's testimony on earth, his spiritual knowledge must come from power. Otherwise, it is of no avail. The only kind of knowledge that has spiritual value is the knowledge that comes from Christ as our power. It is easy for us to take the knowledge we have heard as our own and convey it to others, but this has no spiritual value. May the Lord be merciful to us! However, when we find out what power is before the Lord and acquire some spiritual experience, it is easy for us to become disobedient. It is easy for us to think that we know what others do not know, and that we can do many things. Immediately our self is exposed. At this point, God turns our attention to His house. God's house demands our obedience. If we act according to our own will, we cannot live in God's house. When we see the life of the Body, we see our place in it, and we will not overstep. A person who has received God's revelation of the Body of Christ will not act independently. If we truly see the life of the Body, we will see that there is restriction in the house of God, and we will not move freely. At the same time, if we have the life of the Body, we will spontaneously fellowship with other children of God, and we will treasure this fellowship and not feel that it is a burden to us. If God's children do not know the meaning of God's house, they will not be able to fellowship with God's other children. Whoever cannot honor the other brothers and cannot render them their due respect, praise, and position has not seen the house of God. If our natural life has been dealt with, and if we know what the life of the Body means, we will learn to treasure the other brothers and to touch life and receive help in the meetings. We often receive help and touch life when we come to the meetings. Yet when we leave the meeting, another brother may come and tell us that the meeting was terrible and wrong. Actually, what was terrible and wrong was not the meeting but the brother; he did not take his stand in the house of God. As a result, he could not fellowship with others and could not receive the supply of life from others. If his flesh is dealt with, he will see the Body of Christ and spontaneously fellowship with others. He will find that even the weakest brother or sister can render him some help.

These are the characteristics of Canaan. Among all of Abraham's experiences, God chose these three places for him to build altars. This means that God's acceptance, approval, hope, and countenance are upon these three places.

ABRAHAM BEING TRIED

After Abraham arrived in Canaan, the Bible shows us that he was tested three times concerning the land of Canaan. Let us consider these three tests one by one.

The First Test—Famine

Soon after Abraham reached Bethel, failure set in. This was God's dealing to show him that his calling was of God's mercy and was not due to his own goodness. Abraham was not born good; he failed just as everyone else does. Genesis 12:9 says, "And Abram journeyed, going on still toward the south." This was his failure: God had brought him to the house of God, but he did not stay there for long. Instead he moved gradually to the south. Although he did not move immediately into Egypt, he was in the south at the border of Egypt.

When he moved to the south, he encountered a famine. Verse 10 says, "And there was a famine in the land: and Abram went down into Egypt to sojourn there; for the famine was grievous in the land." Abraham had reached the border of Egypt, and it was very easy for him to go into Egypt. After he arrived in Egypt, he began to lie and was rebuked by Pharaoh. There he suffered great shame (vv. 11-20). After this he returned to Canaan. This was his first test.

How did this test start? God appeared to Abraham in Shechem and said to him, "Unto thy seed will I give this land." God intended to give Canaan to him. Did he want it? Abraham was not a strong man. Although God promised to give him this land, Abraham did not maintain his stand. What did he do? He kept moving to the south until he reached Egypt. This was the cause of the first test. The first trial tested Abraham to see if he wanted this land. Abraham did not see the preciousness of the land. In order to establish him in the land, God had to test Abraham.

After his failure in Egypt, Abraham learned one lesson: He realized the importance of Canaan and knew that it was wrong to lie or deceive. It was a shame for God's people to be rebuked by the Egyptians. What did he do? Genesis 13:1-3 says, "And Abram went up out of Egypt, he, and his wife, and all that he had, and Lot with him, into the south. And Abram was very rich in cattle, in silver, and in gold. And he went on his journeys from the south even to Bethel, unto the place where his tent had been at the beginning, between Bethel and Hai." He returned to his former position. Now Abraham knew how to treasure the land. In this land there was no need to lie, and he did not need to bear the reproach of the Egyptians. In this land he could glorify God.

The Second Test—Lot's Choice of the Land

After Abraham returned to Canaan, he encountered the second test. The first test was to see how much Abraham valued and treasured the land. After he learned the lesson of defeat in Egypt, he realized that Canaan was the only place of value, and he returned. After his return it was easy for him to exercise his fleshly hands to hold on to Canaan. Therefore, there was a second test. Genesis 13:5-7 says, "And Lot also, which went with Abram, had flocks, and herds, and tents. And the land was not able to bear them, that they might dwell together: for their substance was great, so that they could not dwell together. And there was a strife between the herdmen of Abram's cattle and the herdmen of Lot's cattle: and the Canaanite and the Perizzite dwelt then in the land." God showed Abraham that although he had obeyed half of God's commandment to leave his country, his kindred, and his father's house, he had not yet obeyed the other half; he had not parted with Lot. Hence, God needed to discipline him through Lot.

Verses 8 and 9 say, "And Abram said unto Lot, Let there be no strife, I pray thee, between me and thee, and between my herdmen and thy herdmen; for we be brethren. Is not the whole land before thee? separate thyself, I pray thee, from me: if thou wilt take the left hand, then I will go to the right; or if thou depart to the right hand, then I will go to the left." Now Abraham knew that God's calling was only for him and not for Lot. Brothers and sisters, we must realize that those who have been called to be the ministers cannot bring along those who have not been called by God. Abraham saw God's calling for him to be a minister, and he said to Lot, "Separate thyself, I pray thee, from me: if thou wilt take the left hand, then I will go to the right; or if thou depart to the right hand, then I will go to the left." He would not hold on to the land with fleshly hands; he was willing to let Lot make the choice.

On the one hand, Abraham had to fulfill God's calling. On the other hand, God had to teach him the lesson that there is no need to use fleshly methods to hold on to God's promised land of Canaan. We should take care to learn this lesson well. God gave the land to Abraham, but this does not mean that Abraham could hold on to it with his flesh. We must learn the lesson of trusting in God to preserve that which He has promised us. There is no need for us to try to preserve it with earthly means or fleshly energy.

This was the second test of Abraham. In the end he overcame, and he was able to say to Lot, "If thou wilt take the left hand, then I will go to the right; or if thou depart to the right hand, then I will go to the left." He did not try to preserve anything with his own strength.

Genesis 13:10-12 says, "And Lot lifted up his eyes, and beheld all the plain of Jordan, that it was well watered every where.... Then Lot chose him all the plain of Jordan; and Lot journeyed east: and they separated themselves the one from the other. Abram dwelt in the land of Canaan...." The best portions were chosen by Lot, while Abraham remained in Canaan. All those who know God do not vindicate themselves. If we truly know God, we do not need to vindicate ourselves. If God has given Canaan to us, there is no need for us to hold on to it with our fleshly hands. We have to learn to believe in God, trust in Him, and bear the cross. Although the result of Abraham's faith in God put him on the hilly terrain, he was nevertheless in the land of Canaan. Lot chose the plain but ended up in Sodom.

Here we see that Abraham had made some progress. From this time on, he began to shine! Verses 14 through 17 say, "And the Lord said unto Abram, after that Lot was separated from him, Lift up now thine eyes, and look from the place where thou art northward, and southward, and eastward, and westward: for all the land which thou seest, to thee will I give it, and to thy seed for ever. And I will make thy seed as the dust of the earth: so that if a man can number the dust of the earth, then shall thy seed also be numbered. Arise, walk through the land in the length of it and in the breadth of it; for I will give it unto thee." Once more God established

Abraham in the land. Humanly speaking, a portion of it seemed to have been taken by Lot. But at this juncture, God came and spoke to Abraham. There was no need for Abraham to stretch out his hands to do anything. Canaan was given to him by the Lord, and there was no need to preserve it with fleshly ways. Our vindication comes from our trust in God; it does not depend on our holding on to anything with fleshly means. May the Lord be merciful to us and deliver us from our own hands and our own ways.

Verse 18 says, "Then Abram removed his tent, and came and dwelt in the plain of Mamre, which is in Hebron, and built there an altar unto the Lord." Having passed the second test, Abraham made some progress. He moved to Hebron. We have to realize that God is after a total victory. While Lot was choosing the plain of Jordan, Abraham might have overcome outwardly, but might not have overcome inwardly. Perhaps outwardly he said, "If thou wilt take the left hand, then I will go to the right; or if thou depart to the right hand, then I will go to the left." But inwardly he might have hoped that Lot would act according to his conscience and would not be so shrewd as to take the best portions. Yet God brought Abraham through; he did not just overcome outwardly, but also inwardly. He moved his tent and dwelt in Hebron. He had indeed overcome.

The Third Test—
Rescuing Lot and Rejecting the Riches of Sodom

The second test had passed, and the third test came. Genesis 14:11-12 says, "And they took all the goods of Sodom and Gomorrah, and all their victuals, and went their way. And they took Lot, Abram's brother's son, who dwelt in Sodom, and his goods, and departed." This was the last test Abraham experienced for the sake of the land.

When Abraham heard the news about his nephew's captivity, he did not say, "I knew that he should not have gone to such a place. When he did, surely God's hand was heavy upon him." What did Abraham do? Verse 14 says, "And when Abram heard that his brother was taken captive, he armed his trained servants, born in his own house, three hundred and eighteen, and pursued them unto Dan." This shows that Abraham was truly an overcomer. He overcame his self and was brought to the point where he no longer had any personal feelings. It did not matter how Lot had treated him; he still recognized Lot as his brother. Although Lot had never overcome, he was still Abraham's nephew. Lot was an ordinary man in Mesopotamia, he was an ordinary man when he reached Haran, and he was an ordinary man after he reached Canaan. He even chose the good land for himself and moved to Sodom. Lot had no virtue except his sorrow over the licentious manner of life of the lawless (2 Pet. 2:7-8); he had no testimony other than this one. Yet Abraham still recognized him as his nephew. Only those who stand on the ground of Hebron, that is, the ground of fellowship, can engage in spiritual warfare. In order to have the strength for warfare, we must not harbor any complaint within us. Even if our brother has wronged us, we should still consider him our brother, and we should still pray for him and help him unreservedly. Only this kind of person can have the power to fight the spiritual battle. Abraham fought by standing on this ground. Therefore, he was able to overcome the enemy.

When Abraham defeated the enemy and took back Lot from the hand of the enemy, it would have been very easy for him to become proud. It would have been very easy for him to say to Lot, "I told you so, but you would not listen!" It would have been very easy for him to have had an expression of contempt on his face, as if Lot owed him something for such a deliverance. Yet Abraham did not show any such expression.

After Abraham brought back all the goods, including his nephew Lot and his goods and the women and the people, the king of Sodom went out to meet him at the valley of Shaveh. Melchizedek king of Salem also brought forth bread and wine to meet him. "And the king of Sodom said unto Abram, Give me the persons, and take the goods to thyself" (Gen. 14:21). Abraham had learned the lesson. He did not consider the goods as trophies of his hard-fought battle and that he deserved them. On the contrary, "Abram said to the king of Sodom, I have lifted up mine hand unto the Lord, the most high God, the possessor of heaven and earth, that I will not take from a thread even to a shoe-latchet, and that I will not take any thing that is thine, lest thou shouldest say, I have made Abram rich" (vv. 22-23). He took a certain stand and showed others that, other than Jehovah, no one could give him anything.

Abraham called God "the possessor of heaven and earth"! We should not think lightly of this title. This means that because of Abraham's stand for the Lord, heaven became the Lord's, and the earth became the Lord's. God was no longer the Lord of heaven only, but the possessor of heaven and earth! Abraham did not invent the title "the possessor of heaven and earth"; he learned this from Melchizedek. After he slaughtered Chedorlaomer and the other kings, he met Melchizedek at the valley of Shaveh, which was the king's dale. After he won the victory, he did not meet others at the height of the city wall, but at the bottom of a humble valley. Melchizedek came to him with bread and wine and blessed him, saying, "Blessed be Abram of the most high God, possessor of heaven and earth: and blessed be the most high God, which hath delivered thine enemies into thy hand" (vv. 19-20). Because a man stood on earth for God, Melchizedek was able to proclaim God as the possessor of heaven and earth. This is the first time in the Bible that God was called the possessor of heaven and earth. After Abraham won the victory on earth, God was called the possessor of heaven and earth!

Abraham had passed through all the tests. In the end he overcame! This was God's work on Abraham. Blessed be the most high God, the possessor of heaven and earth!

CHAPTER FOUR

ABRAHAM AND HIS SON

(1)

Scripture Reading: Rom. 4:3, 17-22; Gal. 4:23-26, 28; Gen. 15:1—16:4a, 15-16

GOD'S PROMISE AND ABRAHAM'S FAITH

The matter of Canaan was settled for Abraham, but from Genesis 15, we see the matter of his son. This does not mean that Canaan is no longer an issue after chapter fifteen. It only means that the focus is no longer on Canaan, but on the seed.

God's Promise

Genesis 15:1 says, "After these things the word of the Lord came unto Abram in a vision, saying, Fear not, Abram: I am thy shield, and thy exceeding great reward."

It was very meaningful for God to reassure Abraham with such a word even though he had just come back from a victory. We have to realize that Abraham was only a man, and his victory was the victory of a man; it was not a superhuman victory. Although God granted him a victory, He did not make him superhuman. It was easy for Abraham to refuse the riches of Sodom when he had the enjoyment of the bread and the wine from Melchizedek; it was easy for him to deny everything then. But after the moment of victory, when the excitement and uproar were over, and when he began to contemplate in his tent, he would undoubtedly worry about how he had offended the four kings by saving Lot, and how he had offended the king of Sodom by declining his goods. It was unavoidable for him to have some fear. We can detect this from God's word to Abraham. God always has a reason when He speaks. God said, "Fear not," because Abraham was afraid. God gave him two reasons to not fear: (1) "I am thy shield;" no one could attack him anymore. (2) "I am...thy exceeding great reward"; therefore, whatever Abraham lost he could find in Him. God was comforting Abraham.

Verse 2 says, "And Abram said, Lord God, what wilt thou give me, seeing I go childless, and the steward of my house is this Eliezer of Damascus?" Abraham told the Lord that his problem was not that simple. It seemed as if he turned the question back to the Lord: "Lord, don't You know?" The Lord likes to hear us speak. On the one hand, the Lord wants us to fear Him. On the other hand, He likes to hear us speak. When God speaks, we listen. When we speak, God listens. Abraham was telling God that his problem was not one of goods, but of a son. The matter of Canaan had been settled. Now there was the problem of a son. He said, "What wilt thou give me, seeing I go childless, and the steward of my house is this Eliezer of Damascus?" This man from Damascus was not begotten of him; he was not Abraham's son. Although Abraham had heard God say, "I will make of thee a great nation" and "I will make thy seed as the dust of the earth," and although the matter of Canaan was settled, he still had no son!

God is teaching us a lesson here. Does He not know everything? Did He not know Abraham's need for a son? Yes, God knows, but He likes to see us being His friends. He wants us to enter into His heart and His mind, and He wants us to speak to Him this way. Abraham entered into God's mind in this way. God had promised him a son, but He wanted Abraham to ask for it himself. Abraham was saying that if God wanted a nation, He had to give him a son, and the son had to be born of his own house, rather than from somewhere else. The nation had to be brought in through one begotten of him, not through one bought by him. The nation should belong to his sons, not to his servants. Abraham realized that none of his three hundred eighteen trained servants nor Eliezer of Damascus could solve this problem. He needed someone begotten of him. Only someone begotten of him could solve the problem. This was what he meant when he spoke with

God. Abraham was indeed a friend of God! He had entered into God's heart! Without a son, the land would have been vain and the promise would have been useless to Abraham! Without a son he could have never received the blessings. This realization was a result of God's work in Abraham.

After Abraham spoke, God did not immediately answer. He allowed Abraham to go on speaking. God is a God who is very good at listening. Verse 3 says, "And Abram said, Behold, to me thou hast given no seed: and, lo, one born in my house is mine heir."

Abraham Justified by Faith

Verses 4 through 6 say, "And, behold, the word of the Lord came unto him, saying, This shall not be thine heir; but he that shall come forth out of thine own bowels shall be thine heir. And he brought him forth abroad, and said, Look now toward heaven, and tell the stars, if thou be able to number them: and he said unto him, So shall thy seed be. And he believed in the Lord; and he counted it to him for righteousness." This is the first time the Bible speaks of faith. Abraham is the father of faith. He believed God's word in a definite way, and God counted it to him for righteousness.

God told Abraham, "He that shall come forth out of thine own bowels shall be thine heir." This shows us that God's goal is not achieved through the many people He has gathered, but through those whom He has begotten. Those who are not begotten of God do not count; they cannot fulfill God's purpose. God's eternal purpose is fulfilled through those whom He has begotten.

God asked Abraham if he could count the stars in heaven and told him that his descendants would be as numerous as the stars. Abraham believed in God, and God counted it to him for righteousness. As we have mentioned previously, God first had to work on one person and gain something in him before He could gain something through many others. In order for God to have many believers, He first had to gain one believer. Abraham believed in God, and God counted it to him for righteousness.

THE WAY OF THE CROSS

We have to pay attention to the following words: "And he said unto him, I am the Lord that brought thee out of Ur of the Chaldees, to give thee this land to inherit it. And he said, Lord God, whereby shall I know that I shall inherit it?" (Gen. 15:7-8). In the beginning God said to him, "I am thy shield, and thy exceeding great reward." But Abraham said to the Lord, "I go childless." God then told him that only he who came forth out of his own bowels would be his heir, and that his seed would be as the stars in heaven. Then he asked God for more proof. He wanted to know how he could be assured that the land would be his inheritance. Abraham believed God's promise, and God acknowledged his faith. His question was not a indication of unbelief, but a request for a sign for his faith. In answering this question, God shows the believers His way of reaching His goal.

How did God answer him? Verses 9 and 10 say, "And he said unto him, Take me a heifer of three years old, and a she goat of three years old, and a ram of three years old, and a turtledove, and a young pigeon. And he took unto him all these, and divided them in the midst, and laid each piece one against another: but the birds divided he not." Verse 12 says, "And when the sun was going down, a deep sleep fell upon Abram; and, lo, a horror of great darkness fell upon him." Verses 17 and 18 say, "And it came to pass, that, when the sun went down, and it was dark, behold a smoking furnace, and a burning lamp that passed between those pieces. In that same day the Lord made a covenant with Abram, saying, Unto thy seed have I given this land, from the river of Egypt unto the great river, the river Euphrates." This was God's answer.

Abraham "divided them in the midst, and laid each piece one against another. . . . behold a smoking furnace, and a burning lamp that passed between those pieces." This is the proof. It is a picture of the way of the cross. What does it mean to divide "in the midst"? To divide in the midst is to die; it is the cross. What does it mean to pass "between the pieces"? To pass "between the pieces" is to die, which also means to pass through the cross. God showed Abraham that his inheritance

of the land was based on the work of the cross, and that his
seed was able to stand in this land through the death of the
cross.

We have to realize that the cross is the foundation of all
spiritual living. Without passing through the cross, we cannot
live for God on this earth. Even if we can give a message on
the cross, it will not produce any spiritual effect unless we are
first dealt with by the cross. Only those who have passed
through the cross will have the smoking furnace and the
burning lamp. In other words, only those who have passed
through death will have the purging, cleansing, and genuine
light.

The problem with many people is that whenever they find
themselves with a little power or a little achievement in the
work, they think that they are useful in God's hand. Actually,
there is not such a thing. The whole matter depends on the
kind of substance you bring into the Lord's work. If you bring
something of yourself into the work, you have failed already.
You have not failed because you cannot speak, you are not
powerful enough, or you are not familiar enough with the
Scripture. You have failed because you are the wrong person.
The cross has not done its work in you. We have to be clear
that only those who have passed through the cross will
inherit the land. Those who have not passed through death
will not inherit the land. We need the purifying work. How
difficult it is to be pure in the Lord's work! What does it mean
to be pure? To be pure means to be without any mixture. In
our work for the Lord, how easy it is to say one word in the
spirit and the next word in the flesh. How easy it is to say one
word by the Lord and the next word by ourselves. This is mixture, and this is impurity. Consequently, we need the Lord to
bring a smoking furnace to pass through the pieces in order
to conduct a purifying work in us. The efficacy of the death of
Christ will make us a pure person. The Lord does not want us
to be a mixed person. He wants to purge us so that we may be
pure.

What passed through the pieces was not only a smoking
furnace but also a burning lamp. Before there is the smoking furnace, there must first be the cross, and before there

is the burning lamp, there must also be the cross. Hence, in order to have real light, one must first pass through death. A person who has not passed through death may be very clever and knowledgeable; others may think that his words are very intelligent. But such a person does not possess any piercing light. The burning lamp, the genuine light, comes from the cross. It comes from the act of passing through the pieces, that is, from passing through death. No one can fulfill the ministry of God's work based on his human wisdom or knowledge. In order to fulfill such a ministry, one must have the experience of the cross before the Lord. It is easy to preach the doctrine of the cross, but these verses show us that only those who know and experience the cross can stand for God.

After Abraham divided everything in the midst and laid each piece one against another, he fell asleep. Suddenly a great darkness fell upon him. A person who does not know the cross will think that he is more than qualified to work for the Lord and that there is nothing to be fearful of, but a person who knows the cross will see great darkness falling upon him. He will realize that he can do nothing and that he is totally incapable of doing anything by himself. When a person is brought by the Lord to the place of weakness and when he feels that he cannot do anything and is not worthy of doing anything, he can begin to work for the Lord. When we truly see that this work is the Lord's work and that we are useless and when we truly see the Lord's holiness and our filthiness, the Lord will begin to use us.

How did Abraham inherit the land? God showed him that he had to pass through death; he had to pass through the cross. Only by going through the way of the cross will we inherit the land, and only then will we be able to live for God continuously on this earth.

"THY SEED"

Genesis 15:5 says, "And he brought him forth abroad, and said, Look now toward heaven, and tell the stars, if thou be able to number them: and he said unto him, So shall thy seed be." The word "seed" refers to his descendant. It is singular, not plural, in number. This is very strange because humanly speaking, if his descendants were to be as numerous as the stars in heaven, "seed" should have been plural. But when God was telling Abraham of the multiplicity of his descendants, He used the word "seed" in the singular. Why does He use the singular form of the word? Who was the one seed? In Galatians 3:16, Paul said, "He does not say, 'And to the seeds,' as concerning many, but as concerning one: 'And to your seed,' who is Christ." Hence, the seed that God referred to was not many people, but one person. This person was not Isaac, but Christ.

This shows us that the One who inherits the land is the one seed. As far as Abraham was concerned, the seed was Isaac. But in a wider context, the seed is Christ. Isaac was just a shadow; the substance is Christ. In other words, Christ will inherit the land and bless the earth. Both power and authority are with Christ. God's work of recovery is carried out by Christ, not by Isaac.

The matter of sonship is very important. If this matter of sonship and the seed is not settled, no one can carry out God's recovery work. If Abraham was not brought to the point of perfection, he could not have brought in Isaac. Abraham first had to become a vessel before Isaac could be brought in. This means that the glorious Christ will be brought in only when a group of people believe as Abraham believed; only then will God's work be accomplished. Isaac was merely a shadow; the reality is Christ. In the same way, Abraham was a shadow; the reality is the church. Just as Abraham became a vessel to bring in Isaac, so the church is a vessel to bring in the glorious Christ.

God wanted Abraham to become a vessel to bring in Isaac. The descendants of Abraham will fulfill God's purpose; Abraham himself did not fulfill God's purpose. Hence, the church is nothing in itself. What is important is that the church brings in Christ and expresses Christ on earth for the recovery of all God's work on earth. Abraham was a vessel to bring in Isaac. Today the church is a vessel to bring in Christ.

THE FIRST TEST—
THE BIRTH OF ISHMAEL

It is not a simple thing to usher in Isaac. Abraham had to be tested. In order for us to be God's vessel, bring in Christ, and express His authority, there must be many tests. After Genesis 15, the Bible shows us that Abraham was tested three times concerning his son just as he was tested three times concerning the land of Canaan. Two of these tests occurred before the birth of his son, and one occurred after his birth. All three tests prepared Abraham for the ushering in of Isaac. In other words, the church must be tested and prepared before it can bring back the glorious Christ to the earth.

Chapter fifteen tells us that Abraham said to the Lord, "God, what wilt thou give me, seeing I go childless, and the steward of my house is this Eliezer of Damascus?" God said, "He that shall come forth out of thine own bowels shall be thine heir." Abraham believed in God, and God counted it to him for righteousness. The promise of begetting a son was there, and the faith was there. However, day after day, there was no son. Month after month, there was no son, and year after year, there was no son. This shows us that faith has to be tested. Abraham's faith grew step by step.

Genesis 16:1 says, "Now Sarai, Abram's wife, bare him no children." He was now eighty-five years old. His wife Sarah could not bare him a son. What should he do? At that juncture, his wife said to him, "Behold now, the Lord hath restrained me from bearing: I pray thee, go in unto my maid; it may be that I may obtain children by her" (v. 2). What did Abraham do? "Abram hearkened to the voice of Sarai. And Sarai, Abram's wife, took Hagar her maid the Egyptian... and gave her to her husband" (vv. 2-3). The Bible specifically says that "Abram had dwelt ten years in the land of Canaan" (v. 3). When Abraham first arrived in Canaan, God promised, "Unto thy seed will I give this land" (12:7). Just before these events God promised him again, "He that shall come forth out of thine own bowels shall be thine heir." By the time he was eighty-five years old, however, he still had no son. He became anxious. In order to have a son, he went in unto Hagar as his concubine. Hagar became pregnant and brought forth Ishmael. The Bible specifically says, "And Abram was four-score and six years old, when Hagar bare Ishmael to Abram" (16:16).

This is a great matter. God ordained that Abraham would beget a son, but His ordination was for Abraham to beget a son through Sarah and that he would beget him at the age of one hundred. However, Abraham shortened the time by four-teen years with his own effort. Moreover, the son was begotten through Hagar. This was the first test that Abraham faced concerning his son.

He believed in God's word. He believed that God would give him a son. Yet he did not realize that believing meant to stop his own activities and wait on God's work! As soon as we believe, we should stop our own work. Hebrews 4:10 says, "For he who has entered into His rest has himself also rested from his works, as God did from His own." When we believe, we should not make haste. Whenever we believe, we should be at rest. Abraham believed in God, yet he did not learn his lesson. He did not see that if he had believed, he should have waited and should not have done anything by himself. He thought that in order to believe, he should help God and do something by himself. Consequently, he accepted his wife's word, took Hagar to be his concubine, and bore Ishmael. Abraham gave God a hand! He thought that since God had promised a son, he would fulfill God's will by doing this! He did not do anything else. All he did was act on his own concerning something that God had promised him. But this one act brought about his failure!

The Principle of Promise
and the Principle of Ishmael

It was not a question of whether Abraham should have a son. It was a question of through whom the son should be begotten. God's heart could not be satisfied with Abraham just having a son. The son of Abraham had to be begotten through Sarah before God's heart could be satisfied. This was the point of contention between God and Abraham.

This is also a point that confuses many Christians today. Many people ask, "Is it wrong for me to preach the truth?" God's Word says that we should testify and preach the gospel. These things are good. But God is concerned with who is doing the work. Who is doing the preaching? It is right to beget sons, but the real question is who is begetting them. God's emphasis is not on whether something has happened, but on what the source is. Often our attention is just on the correctness of the results and the forms. Whatever we think is correct is taken to be correct, and whatever we think is right is taken to be right. However, God is concerned with where something comes from and who is doing it. It is not enough to say that something is the will of God. One must still ask who is fulfilling this will. It is God's will to have a son, but who is going to give birth to this son in order to fulfill His will? If the begetting is done through one's self-effort, the result is Ishmael.

God intended that Abraham be the father. Therefore, He did a special work on him in order to show him what it means for God to be the Father. For God to be the Father means that everything should issue from God. If Abraham did not see that everything issued from God and that He is the Father, he would not have been qualified to be the father of many nations. Yet the begetting of Ishmael issued from Abraham himself and was not from God.

The greatest test to God's children is in the choosing of the source for their work. Many of God's children often say that such and such a thing is "good," "right," or "according to God's will." But behind these "good" and "right" things that are "according to God's will," the self is doing all the work, and there is no realization of the cross and no ground given to God to deal with the fleshly life. Under these conditions they do God's will by performing many so-called good and right things. The result is not Isaac, but Ishmael. We have to ask God to speak to us and show us who is actually doing these things. This is the critical issue. We may work in a certain place, labor diligently, and save many souls, but in the final analysis, the number of souls that are saved and the appearance of the work are not important. Whether we have done something by God or by ourselves is what is important. The most regrettable thing that we can do is to teach God's Word, preach God's truth, and exercise God's gift by ourselves. If we have done this, we should bow down our head and confess our sins. We have to realize that the works done "for His sake," which are not of Him, and which are done without recognizing Him as the Father, have no spiritual value at all. God must bring us to such a point. Whether or not our spiritual work is pure depends on how much of the work comes out of God and how much of it comes out of the self.

Since Abraham wanted a son, he should have realized that God is the Father and should have allowed Him to be the Father, laying himself aside. Abraham wanted Isaac, but he should not have tried to beget him by himself. In other words, if we want Christ to inherit the land and if we want to stand for God, we should not try to bring Him in by ourselves. We should not act or do anything by ourselves. We have to put ourselves aside. This is the greatest and hardest test. This is where God's servants most frequently fail. We must remember that God's work must not only be free from sin, it must be free from our own efforts as well. God is not only asking how well a work is done, but who is doing the work. Unfortunately, it is easy to exhort men to forsake sin, but it is not easy to exhort men to forsake self-effort. May God bring us to the point where we can say to the Lord, "I want to do Your will! You are within me and You must enable me to do Your will. I am not here to do Your will by myself! It must be You, not I!"

We must remember that "My thoughts are not your thoughts, / And your ways are not My ways, declares Jehovah. / For as the heavens are higher than the earth, / So are My ways higher than your ways, / And My thoughts higher than your thoughts" (Isa. 55:8-9). Therefore, anything we do by ourselves, even though it may be good in our eyes, cannot satisfy God's heart. Even carrying out His will by ourselves will not satisfy His heart. The only thing that will satisfy His heart is that which is done by Himself alone. Although He has lowered Himself and is willing to use us, we have to remember that we are merely servants whom He uses as vessels in His hand. We cannot replace Him in anything. We can only allow God to work through us; we cannot do anything by ourselves. Eventually, Isaac was born of Abraham, but Isaac was the son born according to God's promise. It was God who caused Isaac to be born. God begot this son through Abraham. The principle of promise is totally different from the principle of Ishmael. May the Lord be merciful to us and deliver us from the principle of Ishmael.

Grace and the Law

Abraham married Hagar and begot Ishmael. Galatians 4 says that "the one of the maidservant was born according to the flesh...from Mount Sinai, bringing forth children unto slavery, which is Hagar. Now this Hagar is Sinai the mountain in Arabia..." (vv. 23-25). In other words, Hagar represents the law. What is the law? The law represents God's demand. The Ten Commandments represent God's demands on man. God wants this and He wants that. What does it mean to keep the law? Keeping the law means giving something to God and pleasing God.

But Galatians 3:10 says, "Cursed is everyone who does not continue in all the things written in the book of the law to do them." In other words, those who say, "I will please God," are cursed. Why are they cursed? It is because man cannot please God by himself, and he is not qualified to please God (Rom. 8:7-8). In the Bible the law is frequently mentioned in conjunction with the flesh. Romans 7 is a chapter particularly on the law. It is also a chapter particularly on the flesh. What is the flesh? Simply put, the flesh is self-effort; the flesh is the self. Whenever we try to keep the law, we are in the flesh. Whenever man tries to please God by his own effort, the law comes. A person who tries to please God with the fleshly strength is one with whom God is not pleased. This is what Hagar and Ishmael represent. Hagar represents the law, while Ishmael represents the resulting flesh.

Abraham was a believer. He tried to please God and fulfill

God's goal. God wanted him to have a son, and he tried to have a son by himself. Was this not according to God's will, and did he not do it to please God? Could it be wrong? However, Paul said, "The one of the maidservant was born according to the flesh." It is true that God's will should be done. But the question is who should be the one to do His will. If we try to do His will by ourselves, the result is Ishmael. Abraham was wrong, not in his goal but in his source. His goal was to see God's promise being fulfilled, but he was wrong to fulfill it by his own strength.

Now we are clear. Not only will God reject those who do things that are not pleasing to Him. He will reject even those who do things that are pleasing to Him, but who do them according to themselves. We will not please God if we sin, and neither will we please God if we try to do good by our flesh. Whether or not we please God depends on whether the cross has done its work in dealing with our flesh and the natural life. Are we saying, "God, I cannot do anything, and I am not qualified to do anything; I can only look to You"? A person who truly believes in God is one who does not act according to his flesh. God is the Master of the work. The thing that offends God the most is usurping His place in the work. This is often where our mistake lies. We cannot believe, we cannot trust, and we cannot wait. We cannot commit everything to God. This is the root of our offense against God.

God ordained that Abraham would beget a son through Sarah. Galatians 4:23 tells us that "the one of the free woman was born through promise." The free woman was Sarah. Hagar represents the law, while Sarah represents grace. What is the difference between law and grace? Doing things by ourselves is law, while grace is God doing things for us. Simply put, grace is God doing everything for us. If we are doing it, it is not grace. Only when God is doing it for us is it grace. Grace, as defined in the Bible, is not forbearance or tolerance, nor is it doing anything by ourselves. It is something specific that God does in us. The specific work God wanted to do in Abraham was begetting Isaac through Sarah. Isaac was to be begotten of Abraham, but he was to be begotten through grace and through God's promise.

No Life without Death

Genesis 16 says that Abraham begot Ishmael when he was eighty-six years old. At that time his fleshly energy and natural strength still existed. This is why Galatians 4 says that Ishmael was born of the flesh. Genesis 21 tells us that by the time Abraham begot Isaac, he was already a hundred years old (v. 5). Romans 4 tells us that when he was about a hundred years old, Abraham considered his own body as already dead and Sarah's womb as being deadened (v. 19). In other words, his fleshly energy and natural strength were gone. Abraham did not have any more strength to beget a son, and neither did Sarah. God chose this time for Isaac to be born. This means that God wanted Abraham to consider himself as a dying, and even dead, person so that he could trust in the God who gives life to the dead and calls the things not being as being. God's intention was for Abraham to realize that he was not the Father. It is very interesting that God wanted him to be a father, yet at the same time, He wanted him to see that he was not the Father. He waited until all the natural energy of Abraham was gone before He gave him Isaac.

This is the kind of work that God wants to perform in us. He is always waiting. Even if it means waiting for fourteen years, He will still wait. He is waiting for the day when we realize that we cannot make it, and when we see ourselves as good as dead. Then we will beget Isaac. He cannot use us today because our time has not come. God is after not only the accomplishment of His will, but an accomplishment that issues from Him. If we only have doctrines and knowledge and have never been brought to the point where we tell Him, "I am through, I am dead, and I cannot make it," He cannot use us, and we cannot beget Isaac or fulfill His goal.

One very important condition for begetting Isaac is the matter of time. The Lord cannot really use us and we cannot really manifest Christ or uphold God's testimony on earth until we are a hundred years old. This is the time when everything about us is finished. Before that day arrives, every work that we do by ourselves is Ishmael.

The question now is whether we want Ishmael or Isaac. It is easy to beget Ishmael; if we are like Hagar, we can beget Ishmael at any time. It is easy to do things through Hagar. If we are like Hagar, there is no need for us to wait, but if we would be like Sarah, there is a need for us to wait. In begetting Ishmael, one does not need to wait. But in order to beget Isaac, there is the need of waiting. One has to wait for God's promise, for His timing, and for Him to do the work. Those who cannot wait for God to work, who will not allow God to work, and who do not have God working for them will stretch out their own hands to seize Ishmael. Those who want to have Isaac must wait on God. The day will come when we cannot do anything by ourselves, when we are not able to do anything, are not capable of anything, and are completely through in ourselves. That will be the day when Christ will be fully manifested in us and God's goal will be fulfilled. Before that time, everything that we do by ourselves will have no spiritual value; rather, it will be harmful. In spiritual work it is not a matter of how much we do, but a matter of how much we have gained of the Lord's work. In spiritual matters, God's work and man's work are two entirely different things. There is a vast difference between the value of God's work and the value of man's work. Only that which comes out of Him has any spiritual value. Anything that does not come out of Him has no spiritual value.

What then is Ishmael? Ishmael is anything born prematurely. It is doing things by oneself. We can say that Ishmael includes two characteristics: the first is a wrong source, and the second is a premature timing. In spiritual things nothing tests us more than the matter of time. It often does not take much for our flesh to be exposed. All that God needs to do is put us aside for three months, and our flesh will not be able to stand it. But God will never be pleased to see an Ishmael before His time. Even if we can say a few words or do a few things, and even if these things appear to be of God, He will not be pleased with them. God's goal must be achieved according to God's time and through God's power. This is the principle of Isaac—a principle of God's time and God's power.

Abraham Being Justified Once Again

Romans 4:19-22 says, "And not weakening in his faith, he considered his own body as already dead, being about a hundred years old, as well as the deadening of Sarah's womb; but with regard to the promise of God, he did not doubt in unbelief, but was empowered by faith, giving glory to God and being fully persuaded that what He had promised He was able also to do. Therefore also it was accounted to him as righteousness."

We should note that Abraham's justification by faith in these verses is different in time from that spoken of in Romans 4:3, which says, "Abraham believed God, and it was accounted to him as righteousness." This is Paul's quotation of Genesis 15:6. It refers to the time before Abraham was eighty-five years old. At that time God spoke to Abraham in a vision: "He that shall come forth out of thine own bowels shall be thine heir." God also brought Abraham forth abroad and asked him to look toward heaven and number the stars and said to him, "So shall thy seed be." Abraham believed in God, and God counted it to him for righteousness. This was the first justification. Although Abraham believed, his faith was not perfect, and later he begot Ishmael by his own flesh. The words "it was accounted to him as righteousness" in Romans 4:22 refer to the incident in Genesis 17. At that time he was ninety-nine years old. Although he considered his own body as being already dead and his wife's womb as being deadened, he did not doubt in unbelief. He fully believed that God would fulfill what He had promised. This was accounted to him as righteousness. Hence, this was a further justification by faith. There was a time lapse of over ten years, but God was still teaching Abraham the same lesson—the lesson of faith. At the beginning, there was Abraham's own element in his faith. After many years he had entirely lost hope in himself, but he was still able to believe. God counted him as righteous based on his faith. God had brought him to the point where he truly believed. This was the result of God's work in him. This shows us that it is not of him who wills, nor of him who runs, but of God who shows mercy (Rom. 9:16). He is the One who initiates the work, and He is the One who carries out the work. May the Lord be merciful to us. May He help us learn the lesson of faith, and may we look to Him alone!

CHAPTER FIVE

ABRAHAM AND HIS SON

(2)

Scripture Reading: Gen. 16:16—18:33; 20:1-2, 10-13, 17-18; 21:1-3, 10; Col. 2:11; Phil. 3:3

Abraham's Circumcision

God promised Abraham a son, but Abraham did not wait on God for his son; he married a concubine and gave birth to a son—Ishmael. After he begot Ishmael, there was a thirteen-year period in which God did not speak to him (Gen. 16:16—17:1). Although he begot a son, he wasted thirteen years. This is the experience of many Christians. Whenever we act according to the flesh, God puts us aside and allows us to eat the fruit of our flesh. In God's eyes that period of time is a total waste.

After Abraham begot Ishmael, during the long period of thirteen years, there was no peace in his family. However, the Bible does not show us that Abraham had any regret. On the contrary, he treasured Ishmael very much. We can see this from his word to the Lord: "O that Ishmael might live before thee!" (17:18). Although chapter fifteen tells us that he believed, there does not seem to have been too much pursuing on his part. Day after day, he still took satisfaction in Ishmael. According to our thought, if a man has been walking according to the flesh for thirteen years and still has no feeling of guilt, there must not be much hope for him. But we must remember that Abraham was called by God. God had a purpose in him which He had to fulfill; He could not give him up. Although he backslid for thirteen years and although God did not speak to him during all that time, He was working all the time. God does not give up those whom He has chosen. If He wants to gain a person, that person cannot escape His hand. Even though Abraham had failed, God still came and looked for him. We have to realize that no fleshly pursuit, struggle, fretting, or unrest will bring us forward. We should learn to commit ourselves to the hand of the Almighty. He will lead us as He sees fit.

God Making a Covenant with Abraham

After thirteen years, Abraham was ninety-nine years of age and was becoming old. He considered his own body as being already dead. Even if he wanted to have a son, he could no longer do it. Then God appeared to him and said, "I am the Almighty God" (17:1). This was the first time that God revealed His name as "the Almighty God." The name *Almighty God* in the original language can be translated as "all-sufficient God." After God revealed this name to him, He put a demand on him. "Walk before me, and be thou perfect." Although Abraham had believed that God is powerful, he might not have believed that God is all-sufficient. This was why he tried to do things by himself. God showed him that if he believed in God as the all-sufficient One, he had to walk before Him as a perfect man. Being perfect is being pure. God required Abraham to be pure and without any mixture.

After God showed this to Abraham, He said, "I will make my covenant between me and thee, and will multiply thee exceedingly.... My covenant is with thee, and thou shalt be a father of many nations. Neither shall thy name any more be called Abram, but thy name shall be Abraham; for a father of many nations have I made thee.... And I will establish my covenant between me and thee and thy seed after thee in their generations, for an everlasting covenant, to be a God unto thee and to thy seed after thee. And I will give unto thee, and to thy seed after thee, the land wherein thou art a stranger, all the land of Canaan, for an everlasting possession; and I will be their God" (vv. 2-8). God wanted to gain a people through Abraham, and God wanted to be their God.

What kind of a standing should Abraham and God's people take before they can become His people? God said,

"This is my covenant, which ye shall keep, between me and you and thy seed after thee; Every man child among you shall be circumcised" (v. 10). In other words, God wants a people, yet they must not have any fleshly activity, power, or strength. Who then are the people of God? They are those who have been circumcised. Circumcision is the mark of God's people. Those who were eight days old, whether they were born in the house or bought with money of any stranger had to be circumcised (v. 12). It was not enough to be born, and it was not enough to be bought. One had to be circumcised as well. We are all born of God and bought by God. As far as redemption is concerned, we were bought by God. As far as life is concerned, we were born of God. But if we are not circumcised, we will have no part in the testimony of the people of God. God told Abraham, "The uncircumcised man child whose flesh of his foreskin is not circumcised, that soul shall be cut off from his people" (v. 14). Those who were not circumcised were to be cut off from among God's people. This has to do with the testimony. It means that those who are not circumcised cannot be vessels for God's testimony. A man may be redeemed and have life, but if he is not circumcised, and if he does not know the flesh-dealing cross, he cannot be of God's people; he still has to be cut off from the people.

The Meaning of Circumcision

Colossians 2:11 says, "In Him also you were circumcised with a circumcision not made with hands, in the putting off of the body of the flesh, in the circumcision of Christ."

Philippians 3:3 says, "For we are the circumcision, the ones who serve by the Spirit of God and boast in Christ Jesus and have no confidence in the flesh."

These two verses show what circumcision is. Simply put, circumcision is the removal of the flesh. What should be the attitude of those who are circumcised? They should have no confidence in the flesh and should not put their trust in the flesh. (The word "confidence" in Philippians 3:3 can be translated "trust" according to the original language.) Who are the circumcision? They are the ones who serve by the Spirit of

God and who put no trust in the flesh. Therefore, circumcision deals with man's inherent energy, his natural strength.

How appropriate it was for God to say such a word to Abraham! God showed Abraham that whatever he did and begot by himself was just Ishmael. If the flesh is not dealt with, one will have no part in God's covenant. If the flesh is not dealt with, one cannot be of God's people and cannot maintain His testimony or participate in His recovery work.

The greatest problem among God's children is that they do not know what the flesh is! The flesh that many Christians know is merely related to the matter of sin. It is true that the flesh causes us to sin. But the flesh does not cause man to just sin. Romans 8:8 says that "those who are in the flesh cannot please God." This means that the flesh has tried to please God. Many times, the goal of the flesh may not be to try to offend God; its goal may be to try to please God. Romans 7 shows us that the flesh exerts great effort to keep the law, to do good, to do God's will, and to please God. However, it cannot make it. Our experience tells us that it is comparatively easy to deal with the sinning flesh, but it is very difficult to deal with the flesh that tries to please God. This is the flesh that tries to creep into God's work and service. This is the flesh that creeps into all the things of God.

Some people do not realize that man cannot please God by himself. They think that even though they were once a certain kind of person, now they can do good because their goal has changed since they have believed in the Lord. Such people do not realize that God is concerned not merely with changing their goals, but with terminating their flesh. If they want to please God with their flesh, God will tell them that the flesh cannot please Him. We must see that circumcision is the cutting off of the flesh, the very flesh that begets Ishmael, the flesh that tries to please God. Circumcision deals with the flesh that tries to do God's will and to fulfill His promise by itself. This was what God wanted Abraham to understand.

The greatest problem with God's children is that their flesh is not dealt with before the Lord. They believe in the flesh and put their trust in the flesh. The most obvious sign of unchecked flesh is self-confidence. Self-confidence is the characteristic of the flesh. Philippians 3:3 says, "We are the circumcision, the ones who...have no confidence in the flesh." To put no trust in the flesh is to have no confidence in the flesh. All those who have been smitten by the cross are broken. Although their person may remain, they have learned to fear God and no longer put their trust and confidence in themselves. Before a person is dealt with by the Lord, he quickly judges anything that comes his way. He opens his mouth and makes judgments quickly. But after a person has been dealt with by the Lord, he does not judge lightly; he no longer has any confidence. No one who makes quick proposals and believes in his own strength knows the cross. Such a person has never experienced the work of the cross. Once our flesh is circumcised, we will not believe in ourselves any longer. We will not be that full of confidence, and we will not express our opinions easily. Before the Lord, we must see that we are weak, powerless, helpless, and faltering.

God brought Abraham to the point where he realized that his flesh needed to be dealt with, and that the things he did during the past thirteen years were wrong. There was no room in God's promise for him to do or accomplish anything; all he needed to do was believe. At the same time, God showed him that his descendants for generations to come must be circumcised. This is the basic requirement to be God's people. The condition for us to be God's people in practicality is to have the mark of the cross upon our flesh. Circumcision is the mark of God's people. It is the proof of God's people. What is a mark? A mark is a characteristic. God's people have a characteristic, a mark, which is the denial of the flesh, the rejection of confidence in the flesh. God's people are those whose confidence in the flesh has been cut off. They are the ones who have lost confidence in the flesh.

It is a pity that so many Christians are so confident about themselves. They know how to believe in the Lord Jesus, and they know how to be filled with the Holy Spirit. They know how to overcome, and they know how to live the Christian life. It seems that there is nothing that they do not know! They brag again and again about this and that kind of experience that they had on certain days of certain months. It seems that they are lacking in nothing! They may talk about how they fellowship with God and how they communicate with Him. They think that they know what God is saying concerning certain matters. They think that they know God's will concerning many things. They can talk about what God has told them to speak or pray at such and such a place and at such and such a time. To them, it seems as if knowing God's will is the easiest thing on earth! Yet they lack the mark of having "no confidence in the flesh." Such Christians are indeed in need of God's mercy!

The meaning of circumcision is to cut off the confidence of the flesh. It is to cut off the natural strength so that one no longer speaks and walks in a loose way, but instead becomes a fearful and trembling person.

Abraham's Circumcision

After being dealt with by God for so many years, what kind of person did Abraham become? He became a person who had no trust in himself. Then God said to him, "As for Sarai thy wife, thou shalt not call her name Sarai, but Sarah shall her name be. And I will bless her, and give thee a son also of her" (Gen. 17:15-16). God had promised Abraham earlier that "he that shall come forth out of thine own bowels shall be thine heir." At that time Abraham had believed. After more than ten years, God came again and told him that he would have a son through his wife Sarah. What did Abraham do? He was not as bold as before. He did not have the faith that he had before. When he heard God's promise, he "fell upon his face, and laughed, and said in his heart, Shall a child be born unto him that is a hundred years old? and shall Sarah, that is ninety years old, bear?" And he said to God, "O that Ishmael might live before thee!" (vv. 17-18). This means that he had given up hope entirely in himself. He considered his own body as being already dead and Sarah's womb as being deadened. He could not recall how he had believed at the beginning. He might have said, "Perhaps I was young and could believe then. But now, how can I believe anymore?" In man's eyes Abraham had backslidden all the way.

He had backslidden so much that even his faith was seemingly gone.

Actually, the little faith that Abraham had years ago was a faith that was mixed up with the flesh. It was a faith which begot Ishmael with the flesh. For thirteen years God put Abraham aside and brought him to his end so that he would be - purified. It seemed as if Abraham had failed. Yet God was still working on him. We have to remember that God's work may not be with us when we are victorious, and God's work may not be altogether absent from us when we fail. We should commit ourselves to the hand of the ever-living Lord. As long as He has called us and has started His work in us, He will never give up. Even when we are weak and failing, He still carries on His work, and He is still leading us on step by step.

When God repeated to Abraham that his wife Sarah would bring forth a son, he fell upon his face and laughed. Was he laughing at God? No, he was really laughing at himself. It was too impossible of a situation for him. Yet in the midst of such a situation, he believed in God. It is strange that in easy situations, it is hard to believe in God, while in hard situations, it is easy to believe in God. Easy situations do not help a person believe in God. When a man reaches a desperate situation, he truly believes in God. Hence, God always guides us in two ways: He causes us to trust in Him by bringing us to the end in our environment and by bringing our flesh to its end. The lesson from the environment is outward, while the lesson from circumcision is inward. For Sarah's womb to be deadened was an end in the environment; this was something outward. For Abraham to be circumcised was for his flesh to be brought to its end; this was something inward. We must be brought to our end before we can believe in God. If our flesh is dealt with, we will believe in God whether the environment is smooth or difficult.

God does not want a mixed faith, but a pure faith. We should not believe only when things look bright and we have confidence in ourselves. We should believe simply because God has spoken. Abraham could not believe in this way thirteen years previously. But now he was brought to the point where he considered his body as being already dead and his wife's womb as being deadened. The faith which he now had was a pure faith; it was one that believed in God alone. His previous faith was based on God and on himself. His faith now was based on God alone because all his strength was gone, and there was nothing left in him; everything was finished. Abraham's laugh confirms this: To him everything in him was finished. Yet God said to him, "Sarah thy wife shall bear thee a son indeed; and thou shalt call his name Isaac" (17:19).

We should take note of this fact: God wanted Abraham to beget Isaac, not Ishmael! God will never accept any replacement of His work. After He waited for thirteen years, He still wanted Abraham to beget Isaac. Ishmael can never satisfy God's heart!

Genesis 17:23-24 says, "And Abraham took Ishmael his son, and all that were born in his house, and all that were bought with his money, every male among the men of Abraham's house; and circumcised the flesh of their foreskin in the selfsame day, as God had said unto him. And Abraham was ninety years old and nine, when he was circumcised in the flesh of his foreskin." Abraham's circumcision was his acknowledgment that he was through, that his flesh absolutely could not make it. As far as his own condition was concerned, he could not even believe in God's promise. But just when he could not believe anymore, the real faith came in! When he could believe no longer and when he could do nothing anymore, he truly trusted in God. It seemed as if he believed and, at the same time, was unable to believe. There was only a flicker of faith in him. Yet this flicker of faith was the pure faith. Abraham's condition at this time is described in Romans 4:19-20: "And not weakening in his faith, he considered his own body as already dead, being about a hundred years old, as well as the deadening of Sarah's womb; but with regard to the promise of God, he did not doubt in unbelief, but was empowered by faith, giving glory to God."

God's Friend

In chapter eighteen, after Abraham believed and was circumcised, his fellowship with God became more intimate.

This shows that he was indeed a friend of God. Genesis 18 is a special chapter. This chapter speaks of three things: (1) fellowship, (2) knowledge, and (3) intercession. These three things are intimately related, and they are the special enjoyment of a Christian who has been following the Lord for many years. We can only cover them briefly.

"And the Lord appeared unto him in the plains of Mamre" (Gen. 18:1). At the end of chapter thirteen, Abraham was dwelling by the oaks of Mamre, which was in Hebron. Hebron means fellowship. For God to appear to Abraham meant that Abraham was standing on the ground of fellowship. "And he sat in the tent door in the heat of the day; and he lifted up his eyes and looked, and, lo, three men stood by him" (18:1-2). This is a very peculiar portion of the Old Testament. God visited Abraham, not as the God of glory, but in the form of a man. It was as if He came to Abraham in plain clothes. God's appearance was fully in the position of a man. Therefore, Abraham did not feel that it was God who appeared to him. "And when he saw them, he ran to meet them from the tent door, and bowed himself toward the ground, and said, My Lord, if now I have found favor in thy sight, pass not away, I pray thee, from thy servant: let a little water, I pray you, be fetched, and wash your feet, and rest yourselves under the tree: and I will fetch a morsel of bread, and comfort ye your hearts; after that ye shall pass on: for therefore are ye come to your servant. And they said, So do, as thou hast said. And Abraham hastened into the tent unto Sarah, and said, Make ready quickly three measures of fine meal, knead it, and make cakes upon the hearth. And Abraham ran unto the herd, and fetched a calf tender and good, and gave it unto a young man; and he hasted to dress it. And he took butter, and milk, and the calf which he had dressed, and set it before them; and he stood by them under the tree, and they did eat" (vv. 2-8). This was Abraham's fellowship with God. Abraham was led by God to the point where he could communicate with God as a friend!

Then the subject of the son was brought up once more. Chapter seventeen speaks of Abraham laughing. Chapter eighteen speaks of Sarah laughing. Abraham was ready; he could communicate with God. While they were conversing outside the tent, Sarah was listening in the tent door, and while they were speaking to one another, Sarah was laughing within herself. God pointed out Sarah's laughing (vv. 12-15). This was fellowship. God became a man and communicated with a man. This is the fellowship between God and His people.

"And the men rose up from thence...and Abraham went with them to bring them on the way" (v. 16). This is fellowship. This is being God's friend. Once there is fellowship, there is knowledge. This kind of knowledge is not just the knowledge of the Bible but the knowledge of God. When Abraham fellowshipped with God, he acquired a knowledge of God. "And the Lord said, Shall I hide from Abraham that thing which I do?" (v. 17). What a word of intimacy! God was treating Abraham like a friend. Then God said, "Because the cry of Sodom and Gomorrah is great, and because their sin is very grievous, I will go down now, and see whether they have done altogether according to the cry of it, which is come unto me; and if not, I will know" (vv. 20-21). This means that God revealed His secret to Abraham. Before the Lord, Abraham was able to know what other men could not know. God's will is revealed only to those who walk with Him. The preciousness of walking with God lies in the fact that we can know God.

After God told Abraham of this secret, Abraham immediately entered into a work of intercession. Intercession is governed by fellowship; it is also governed by knowledge. With fellowship there is knowledge, and with knowledge there is the burden for intercession. The prayer that Abraham offered was a prayer that issued from his knowledge of God and his sympathy for God. Abraham drew near and said to the Lord, "Wilt thou also destroy the righteous with the wicked?...Shall not the Judge of all the earth do right?" (vv. 23-25). Abraham stood on God's side to pray; his prayer was fully on behalf of God's righteousness. In other words, his prayer was not to move God's heart but to express it. Hence, a prayer that knows God's heart is not a prayer that changes His will, but one that expresses His will. Abraham's prayer was a prayer that knew God's will; it was a prayer that expressed God's will. He was truly God's friend!

THE SECOND TEST—
PRAYING FOR THE HOUSE OF ABIMELECH

Abraham passed his first test. The bringing forth of Ishmael with his fleshly strength was over. Humanly speaking, he had done everything, and Isaac should have been born. But before the incident in chapter seventeen was barely completed, another came along, and he was tested a second time concerning the matter of his son.

Genesis 20:1 says, "And Abraham journeyed from thence toward the south country, and dwelt between Kadesh and Shur, and sojourned in Gerar." Abraham committed the same mistake as he did in Egypt when he called Sarah his sister. After he was rebuked by Pharaoh of Egypt, God brought him back. But in chapter twenty he went to Abimelech of Gerar and committed the same mistake. It is difficult for us to understand this. How could he fall to such a low state after he had reached the peak of fellowship in chapter eighteen? Chapter twenty relates something that was not mentioned in chapter twelve. Abimelech rebuked Abraham, saying, "What hast thou done unto us?...What sawest thou, that thou hast done this thing?" (vv. 9-10). Abraham said, "Because I thought, Surely the fear of God is not in this place; and they will slay me for my wife's sake. And yet indeed she is my sister; she is the daughter of my father, but not the daughter of my mother; and she became my wife. And it came to pass, when God caused me to wander from my father's house, that I said unto her, This is thy kindness which thou shalt show unto me; at every place whither we shall come, say of me, He is my brother" (vv. 11-13). Hence, the root of this matter was not in Egypt, but in Mesopotamia. His failure in Egypt only exposed the root. The root of failure was in Mesopotamia. Therefore, when he went to Gerar, the same thing happened again.

God dealt with Abraham in order to show him that he and Sarah could not be separated. In Mesopotamia he thought that he and Sarah could be separated, and that during times of peril the couple could become brother and sister. Abraham was standing on the ground of faith, while Sarah was standing on the ground of grace. On man's side, it is faith, and on God's side, it is grace. Faith and grace can never be separated from each other; they must always be together. If grace is taken away, there is no faith, there is no people of God, and Christ cannot be brought forth. But Abraham thought that he could be separated from Sarah. The root was planted in Mesopotamia and exposed in Egypt. Now it was exposed again. God was removing the root that had been planted in Mesopotamia. If this matter had not been taken care of, Isaac could not have been brought forth. In order for God's people to maintain His testimony, there is the need for faith and grace. It is not enough to have faith alone, and it is not enough to have grace alone. God showed Abraham that he could not sacrifice Sarah and could not be separated from her.

It is interesting that "the Lord had fast closed up all the wombs of the house of Abimelech, because of Sarah, Abraham's wife" (v. 18). After Abimelech returned Sarah to Abraham, "Abraham prayed unto God: and God healed Abimelech, and his wife, and his maidservants; and they bare children" (v. 17). After this incident, Sarah begot Isaac in chapter twenty-one. This is amazing.

The women in the house of Abimelech could not bear children. Why did they bear children again when Abraham prayed and God healed them? Others could have prayed for this, but Abraham's own wife had never borne a child. How could he pray for the women in the house of Abimelech? This was indeed a difficult thing to do. But in this matter, the root which Abraham had planted in Mesopotamia was dug out by God. He realized that for his wife to bear children was something entirely up to God. While he was praying for the house of Abimelech, probably he did not have any confidence at all in himself. His confidence was in God and not in himself. Now Abraham was fully delivered from himself. He did not have a son, yet he could pray for others to bear children. His flesh had truly been dealt with.

This is the second test Abraham went through concerning his son. He learned the lesson from this test that God is the

Father. Although his wife and the women in Abimelech's house were the same and could not bear children, he prayed for the women of Abimelech's house. He did it because he knew that God is the Father. He knew that power comes from God and not from himself. If God wants to do something, He can do it. With Him nothing is impossible. Abraham had to pay a price to pray for the women of Abimelech's house. The price was himself. What he prayed for was what he himself sought after. God was asking him to pray for something that he had not had for his whole life. God was touching him on this matter. Hence, in praying for the women of Abimelech's house, Abraham ceased all activities of his self. Only one who did not think about himself and did not consider himself could have prayed for the women of Abimelech's house on that day. Thank the Lord that God brought Abraham to the point where he could truly look away from himself. He could do this because he knew God as the Father.

We have to remember that there are two meanings to the name *Father*. God is our Father, and His relationship with the believers is a father-son relationship; this is very intimate. This is something which many Christians realize at the time of their regeneration. But there is still another lesson we have to learn. God is the Father in the persons of the Trinity; everything is of Him. This is the meaning of God the Father. He is the Father of everything, the Father of all things. This is the other meaning of God the Father. Abraham learned this lesson. He could pray for the women of Abimelech's house, not because he had clusters of children in his house, but because he saw that God is the Father. Through the begetting of Ishmael, Abraham learned to know God as the Father. In this incident with Abimelech, he learned to know God as the Father once again. Therefore, after this incident, God fulfilled His promise to Abraham and brought forth Isaac.

CHAPTER SIX

ABRAHAM AND HIS SON

(3)

Scripture Reading: Gal. 4:29-31; 5:1; Heb. 11:17-19; James 2:20-24; Gen. 21:8-10; 22:1-5, 16-18

After Abraham realized that God is the Father through his intercession for the women in Abimelech's house, Sarah bore him a son at God's appointed time. Abraham called his son Isaac. When his son was born, he was a hundred years old (Gen. 21:5).

The Day Ishmael Was Cast Out

The day Isaac was weaned, God spoke a word through Sarah: "Cast out this bondwoman and her son: for the son of this bondwoman shall not be heir with my son, even with Isaac" (v. 10). This was not Sarah's jealousy. Galatians 4:30 shows us that this was God's word through the mouth of Sarah: "For the son of the maidservant shall by no means inherit with the son of the free woman." This means that only one person could fulfill God's goal. This one was Isaac, not Ishmael. Ishmael was the first, not the second. Therefore, he represented Adam, not Christ. "But the spiritual is not first but the soulish, then the spiritual" (1 Cor. 15:46). Those who are of the flesh cannot inherit the kingdom of God; they cannot fulfill God's goal. The second one was Isaac. Therefore, Isaac represented that which is spiritual, he who can inherit God's inheritance and maintain God's testimony.

It is interesting to see that Ishmael was not cast out the day Isaac was born. He was cast out only after Isaac was weaned. Without Isaac, it was impossible to cast out Ishmael. Some brothers and sisters are full of fleshly works and a fleshly walk. When they hear about the flesh and what it means, they dare not do anything any longer, and they cease their work altogether. They do not have Isaac yet. Therefore, when they cast out Ishmael, they cannot do anything. Many Christians have been used to doing things by themselves and according to their fleshly strength. When they stop their fleshly work, they are left with no spiritual work. They did not have anything spiritual before; all they had were fleshly things. When the flesh is stopped, nothing spiritual remains. The principle is that Isaac must be weaned. This means that Ishmael can only be cast out when Isaac is strong enough to be the son and has gained the proper ground.

What does it mean to be cast out? Let us read Galatians 5:1. "It is for freedom that Christ has set us free; stand fast therefore, and do not be entangled with a yoke of slavery again." This means that the Lord Jesus has freed us; He is already living within us. The life we have received is a life of freedom; we have been freed. Therefore, we should not try to *do* anything to please God. Whenever we try to *do* anything, we become Ishmael. Whenever we stop trying, we are living in the freedom of the Son. The Christian life hinges on whether or not something has been done by us. Whenever we try to *do* something to please God, the self and the law of sin and of death come, and we fall back to Ishmael's position and become the sons of a maidservant. As a son of the free woman, there is no need for us to do anything by ourselves. We have a life within us, and this life will do everything in a spontaneous way. We *are* Christians; we do not need to *act out* our Christian life. We *are* children; we do not need to *act like* God's children. We live in what we *are,* not in what we *do.* Whenever we try to *do* something, we are "entangled with a yoke of slavery again" and become sons of the maidservant. If we stand on the ground of Isaac, the life we have will spontaneously be manifested through us.

After Abraham cast out Ishmael, even Abimelech, who had rebuked him once, came to him and said, "God is with thee in all that thou doest" (Gen. 21:22). The root of failure was removed from Abraham, and God was able to fully manifest His own work through Isaac.

THE THIRD TEST—THE OFFERING OF ISAAC

Abraham had been tested twice concerning his son. The first test was in the begetting of Ishmael. The second test was in praying for the women of Abimelech's house. Now he was tested for the third time concerning his son. This third test was the offering up of his son Isaac on Mount Moriah.

Abraham Offering Isaac

Abraham had reached the proper ground. One can say that he had reached the peak, the pinnacle. After chapter twenty-two, the record turns to the story of his old age. Hence, chapter twenty-two marks the peak of Abraham's life. One can say that this was the high noon of his life.

Genesis 22:1-2 says, "And it came to pass after these things, that God did tempt Abraham, and said unto him, Abraham: and he said, Behold, here I am. And he said, Take now thy son, thine only son Isaac, whom thou lovest, and get thee into the land of Moriah; and offer him there for a burnt offering upon one of the mountains which I will tell thee of." This demand had to do with the fulfillment of God's promise. Isaac was Abraham's only son, and he was his beloved. It was a great price for Abraham to offer up Isaac. But this is still not the main point. Hebrews 11 shows us something that Genesis 22 does not record. Hebrews 11:18 says, "In Isaac shall your seed be called." Hence, it was not just a matter of sacrificing Abraham's beloved son, but a matter of God's own promise, goal, and work. God did not give Abraham's son to him alone. His intention was to achieve His goal through Isaac. If Isaac died, what would happen? This was Abraham's test.

This test involved himself as an individual and himself as a vessel. Hebrews 11:18 shows us the aspect of the vessel. God promised to give Abraham a son. Yet He wanted this son to be offered up as a burnt offering! This is something that the flesh cannot stand. A burnt offering must be burned by fire. All of God's promises hinged on Isaac. If Isaac was burned up, would not God's promises be burned up? God's goal and His work were with Isaac. If he was burned up, would not God's promise, goal, and work be burned up as well? It was reasonable and right to cast out Ishmael because he was born of the flesh. But Isaac was born according to God's promise. Why should he be offered up as a burnt offering? Abraham had sought for satisfaction with Ishmael. But God Himself said, "No." It was God who repeatedly said that Sarah would have a son. Abraham did not insist on having this son; it was God who gave this son to him. Now God wanted him back, and not in an ordinary way, but as a burnt offering. This was beyond his comprehension. If Isaac should not have been born, God should have told him sooner. If it was right for Isaac to be born, Abraham should have been able to keep him. If God did not want Abraham to keep Isaac, He should not have given Isaac to him in the first place. If He did want Abraham to have Isaac, He should not have demanded that he be offered up as a burnt offering. What was the purpose of begetting a son and then offering him up? It was solely to bring Abraham into a deeper realization of God as the Father!

God Being the Father

Abraham still had to learn one last lesson. This lesson was actually the lesson he had already learned. In order for God to be the God of Abraham, he had to know God as the Father. There was no question about Isaac; he was indeed given by God and indeed a son according to His promise. But what was Abraham's relationship with Isaac? The deep lesson that we have to learn before the Lord is that we cannot get ourselves directly involved with any of the things that God has given to us. God does not allow us to have a direct relationship with them. It is wrong to acquire something by the flesh, but it is equally wrong to hold on to what is acquired through the promise with fleshly hands. Indeed, Isaac was given by God, but what was Abraham's relationship with Isaac?

In begetting Isaac, Abraham learned that God is the Father. But he still had to learn one more thing. God was the Father before Isaac was born, but was He still the Father after Isaac was born? This is the condition that many Christians face today. Before their "Isaacs" are born, they realize that God is the Father. But after their "Isaacs" are born, their eyes turn to their "Isaacs." They think that their "Isaacs" will fulfill God's promises, accomplish God's goal, and bring in God's work. They think that they have to treasure their "Isaacs," care for their "Isaacs," and raise up their "Isaacs"! God is put aside after their "Isaacs" are born. All of their thoughts are on their "Isaacs," and God becomes nothing to them. However, we have to see that God is the Father. He will not allow our thoughts to be centered on our "Isaacs." God is the Father. He cannot be limited by time. Before Isaac was born, God was the Father. After Isaac was born, God was still the Father. Whether or not God's promises would be fulfilled depended on God, not on Isaac.

Isaac was a gift from God. Here lies our greatest danger before the Lord. Our hands are empty before we receive any gift; thus, we can fellowship and communicate with God. But after we receive the gift, our hands become full, and we do not fellowship or communicate with Him anymore. When our hands are empty, we fellowship with God with empty hands. But when our hands pick up the gift, we become satisfied with the gift in our hands, and we stop fellowshipping with God. God must teach us a lesson: We should put the gifts aside and live totally in God. Before man's flesh is dealt with, he always lives according to God's gift and neglects God Himself. However, this is something that God never endorses.

The begetting of Isaac was one experience that Abraham had. We can say that this was a very precious experience for Abraham. But God does not give us an experience so that we may sit on it for the rest of our lives. We have to realize that our source is God, not experiences. The begetting of Isaac was indeed an experience, but the experience itself was not the Father. It was an experience, but it was not the source. The problem is that once we acquire an experience concerning Christ, we hold on to that experience and treasure the experience, while at the same time, we forget that God is the Father. God will not allow this to happen. He has to show us that our experience can be dropped but He cannot be dropped. Isaac is dispensable, but we cannot be separated from the Father even for a moment.

This still has not touched the crux of the matter. Whether Isaac represents a gift or an experience, this application merely touches our fleshly life. There is another important thing: Isaac represents God's will, which God had spoken to Abraham. If Isaac died, would that not mean that the will of God that was spoken to Abraham would be unfulfilled? Because Abraham cared so much about God's will, he had to use all his energy to hold on to Isaac. This is the situation with many Christians. We have to realize that we are related to God Himself; we are not related to the things which God is about to do. We are not related to the will which He has spoken. We have to be brought to the point where our self no longer exists. We have to be delivered to the point where we want God only, not the things that He wants us to do. We often use fleshly hands to uphold the things that God wants us to do. We think that because God wants us to do a certain thing, we have to try our best to accomplish it. But the lesson that God is really teaching us is to give up our own will so that we will do what God wants us to do and not do what He does not want us to do.

Isaac also represents our spiritual work. God may call us to participate in some kind of spiritual work. However, we may not want to do it. We want our Ishmael, and we have our own work. One day God will speak to us, and after He speaks again and again, we will find that we can no longer escape, and we will say, "All right. I am willing to drop my work to take up Your work." But a second danger follows: We may drop one work only to find ourselves caught up by another. Before we have Isaac, we hold on to Ishmael. After Isaac comes, we hold on to Isaac. We are no longer directly related to God, but related to the work instead. We insist on working and do not give up. We replace God with spiritual works. Therefore, God allows our works to die. We may argue with God, saying, "You asked me to do this. Why have I ended up with such failure?" We have to realize that God allows our work to fail miserably because He does not want us to have any direct relationship with the work. If we see this, our self will go away.

Formerly, the flesh begot Ishmael and not Isaac. Now the

flesh holds on to Isaac. Both are the flesh. God was testing Abraham. He wanted to see if Abraham was directly related to Isaac or directly related to God. This is the test which Abraham faced on Mount Moriah.

Today we have to ask ourselves the same question. God has called us to the work and to serve Him. In the beginning we were unwilling, but later we became willing, and we engaged ourselves in His work. Do we love this work? Are we reluctant to let go of it? Are we holding on to this work with our own hands? If we are, God will come in to deal with us. God wants us to realize that we can sacrifice Isaac but we cannot sacrifice God, because only God is the Father! Yet many Christians only know that they need spiritual works. They do not know that they need God. May the Lord be gracious to us so that we would not be directly related to spiritual works, but directly related to God, because only God is our Father!

God Being the God of Resurrection

By this time Abraham had reached maturity. When he heard that God wanted him to offer up Isaac, he did not feel that this was a difficult thing to do. He told his servant, "Abide ye here with the ass; and I and the lad will go yonder and worship, and come again to you" (Gen. 22:5). He did not even mention the word *sacrifice*. To him this was a worship! Nothing was more precious than God Himself, not even the most important work that He had assigned. Whenever God wanted him to drop something, he willingly dropped it. Everything was for God, and he did not argue with God.

Hebrews 11:19 shows us that at the time Abraham offered up Isaac, he knew that God is the God of resurrection. He obeyed God's command to offer up Isaac, "from which he also received him back in figure." It is true that he did not kill Isaac and that Isaac did not die, but Hebrews 11:19 says that "from which [that is, death] he also received him back in figure." He considered God not only to be the God of creation, but also the God of resurrection. He believed that even if his son died, God would resurrect him. He knew God as the Father, the Initiator of everything, who calls things not being as being and gives life to the dead. He knew that God is the Father, and he believed in God and looked to Him. In Genesis 15 Abraham was justified by faith. God justified him once more because of this act of faith in Genesis 22. James 2:21-23 speaks about this matter. At this point everything with Abraham was directly related to God; he was not related to Isaac in any direct way.

THE COMPLETION OF GOD'S VESSEL

Before the Lord, we have to realize that even the commission we have received, the work we are doing, and the will of God that we know, must be dropped. There is a big difference between what is natural and what is of resurrection. Everything that we do not want to let go of is natural. Everything that comes from resurrection is preserved by God, and we cannot hold on to it with our fleshly hands. We have to learn to thank the Lord for calling us to His work and also learn to thank Him for calling us to not work. We are not directly related to God's work, but to God Himself. Everything should pass through death and resurrection. What is resurrection? Resurrection is anything that we cannot put our hands on, that we cannot hold on to. This is resurrection. Natural things are the things that we can grasp hold of, while we cannot grasp hold of the things in resurrection. We have to see that everything we have is of God and that anything that is of God cannot become our own private possession. We must put it in God's hand. God gave Isaac to Abraham, but Isaac still belonged to God. He did not belong to Abraham. When Abraham reached this point, he became a completed vessel.

When Abraham reached this point, God said, "By myself have I sworn, saith the Lord, for because thou hast done this thing, and hast not withheld thy son, thine only son, that in blessing I will bless thee, and in multiplying I will multiply thy seed as the stars of the heaven, and as the sand which is upon the seashore; and thy seed shall possess the gate of his enemies; and in thy seed shall all the nations of the earth be blessed; because thou hast obeyed my voice" (Gen. 22:16-18). The ultimate goal for which Abraham was called at the beginning was fulfilled. God had called Abraham for three purposes. First, He wanted to give the land of Canaan to Abraham and his descendants. Second, He wanted to make him and his descendants a people of God. Third, He wanted to bless all the nations of the earth through him. Abraham was tested concerning Canaan and concerning his descendant. He became God's vessel, and God was able to say, "In thy seed shall all the nations of the earth be blessed." God's goal was now fulfilled.

Gifts do not constitute God's vessels and ministers. God's vessels and ministers must be those who are before the Lord, who have passed through His dealings, and who have much experience. The greatest misunderstanding we have in our service to God is to think that God's workers are built upon the foundation of knowledge and gifts or even natural cleverness. If a man is naturally clever and has a good memory, others will say that he is quite good and promising in God's service. They will say that he is useful in spiritual matters. Man thinks a vessel is "useful to the Master" as long as he is clever, quick, and eloquent in his natural constitution, as long as he acquires more teachings, theologies, and Bible knowledge, and as long as he has some amount of spiritual gift and eloquence. But we have to say an honest word. The first vessel that God called did not become one because of these things. He was brought through one way. God repeatedly showed him his weaknesses and uselessness and that his fleshly energy was not pleasing to Him. God dealt with him step by step until he truly knew God as the Father. Finally, he offered Isaac to God. By that time, he had become a vessel, and God was able to say, "In thy seed shall all the nations of the earth be blessed."

It is true that there are different levels in our service to God, and we can serve Him wherever we are. But the real question is, "What kind of service should we have in order to satisfy Him?" Those who satisfy God know the cross on the negative side and know God as the Father on the positive side. If our service does not have this knowledge, it lacks spiritual value. May the Lord be gracious to us to show us that everything God did with Abraham was to reveal Himself as the Father and the Initiator of everything. Because Abraham knew God as the Father, he is the only one in the whole Bible who is called "father." Only those who know God as the Father can be a father. What we know of God determines what kind of vessel we are before Him. The God that we know determines the kind of vessel that we are. May the Lord deliver us from dead doctrines and knowledge. We can only be God's vessels and ministers according to our knowledge of Him. God's vessels and ministers are those who know God.

Chapter Seven

THE CHARACTERISTICS OF ISAAC

Scripture Reading: Gen. 25:5-6, 11a; 26:1-5, 23-24

God is not after just Abraham. He is after a corporate vessel. He is after the descendants of Abraham, the church, who will fulfill His purpose. Abraham's history includes both his own experience and the necessary experience of every vessel of God. Abraham was not just an individual; he was the father of those who are of faith (Gal. 3:7). Just as he had to go through these experiences, all those who are of faith must go through the same experiences. In reading the history of Abraham, we have to realize that it is not only a description of Abraham's experience in being dealt with by the Lord, but it is also a description of the standard by which God deals with all of His people. Abraham's experience is God's requirement on every believer. If we do not meet this requirement, we cannot satisfy God's heart, and we cannot reach His goal.

God wants us to be His vessels for the fulfillment of His own plan; He wants us to have a part in His recovery work. Abraham's experiences were wonderful, and the dealings he received were precious. In the beginning he was an ordinary person, but God brought him through many experiences until one day he became a shining and glowing person in Genesis 22. Here a question arises. Why do some of us still not shine even though we have been Christians for many years? If Abraham is the standard of God's people, how can we reach that standard? How can we allow God to accomplish in us what He accomplished in Abraham? God gained a vessel in Abraham. Will He gain a vessel in us? This is the question before us.

. The Bible tells us that God is not only called the God of Abraham, but also the God of Isaac. After this, He is also called the God of Jacob. As far as God's goal is concerned, Abraham was complete in himself. But as far as God's work is concerned, he was not complete. God needed Isaac and Jacob before there could be the completion. This is a very important principle in the Bible. In order for God to gain a person, he must know God as the Father, even as Abraham knew Him as the Father. He must be delivered from the work of the flesh like Abraham was delivered. He must also know God as the God of Isaac and the God of Jacob. A person must know the God of Isaac and the God of Jacob before he can gain what Abraham gained. God's purpose rested entirely on Abraham, and whatever was given to Isaac had been given to Abraham already. Isaac did not go beyond Abraham, and Jacob did not travel further than Abraham. If Abraham touched the peak, why was he not able to inherit a kingdom immediately? He could not because there was still the need of supplementary experiences. There was still the need of Isaac and Jacob to be added to Abraham before God could gain what He intended to gain in Abraham. In other words, we need the experience of Abraham, and we need the experience of Isaac and the experience of Jacob as well. Abraham is a standard for us. But between Abraham and the nation of Israel, there was still Isaac and Jacob. God could not jump over Isaac and Jacob and go directly to the nation of Israel. There first had to be the experiences of the God that Isaac knew and the God that Jacob knew, before there could be the nation of Israel and before there could be the corporate experience. God is after a corporate vessel. In order to be a corporate vessel, one has to know God as the God of Abraham, the God of Isaac, and the God of Jacob. We have to remember God's word continually: "I am…the God of Abraham, the God of Isaac, and the God of Jacob" (Exo. 3:6). As soon as God was called the God of Abraham, the God of Isaac, and the God of Jacob, the nation of Israel appeared. This is revealed in the book of Exodus. Once this point is reached, God has His corporate vessel. Now let us consider the meaning of the God of Isaac.

ISAAC BEING THE SON

We have seen the meaning of the God of Abraham. Abraham himself was a father. On the one hand, God led him to realize that He is the Father. On the other hand, He made Abraham a father. Abraham's original name was Abram, which means "father." Later he was called Abraham, which also means "father," but in a more superlative form; it means the father of many nations. Abraham knew God as the Father, and as a result, he also became a father. He was a father in every sense of the word. As far as God's recovery work is concerned, Abraham was the initiator, and as such he was the father. As far as God's selection is concerned, he was the first to be chosen as one of God's people, and therefore, he was also the father. As far as his acts were concerned, he was the first one to cross the river, and therefore, he was also a father. For two thousand years after Adam, who among all men was a Hebrew? Who did God call to leave his country, kindred, and father's house to go into Canaan? Abraham was the first. Have we heard of anyone who communicated with God and who was so intimate with God that he was called a friend of God? Abraham was the first. Have we heard of anyone who begot a child after passing the age of child begetting? Abraham was the first. Have we heard of anyone who had a son when he was a hundred years old, and who later offered the son as a sacrifice? Abraham was the first. We see from the Bible that many things were first done by Abraham. Indeed, Abraham is the father.

Now that we have seen Abraham as the father, we have to go on to see Isaac as the son. No one's history depicts the Lord Jesus as the Son as much as Isaac's history. Isaac's birth was not according to the flesh but according to God's promise. The first two chapters of Matthew in the New Testament correspond with Genesis in the Old Testament. There was only one person in the New Testament who was not born according to the flesh, and there was only one person in the Old Testament who was not born according to the flesh. Not only was the Lord Jesus born apart from the flesh, but He was an only begotten Son, One who was the beloved of His Father. He was placed on the altar and received back from the altar as the One who had come back from the dead (Heb. 11:19). He is the Son whom God loves, who died and resurrected. His Father also sent a servant to His own country and own kindred to find a wife for Him. Those who study the Bible carefully know that this is the Holy Spirit seeking out the church for Christ. The church is according to the Lord's will; it is begotten of God and belongs to the same household of the Lord Jesus. Isaac and Rebekah were of the same household. God's children, the church, are begotten of God in the same way that the Lord Jesus was begotten of God.

Abraham left Canaan once to go into Egypt, and Jacob spent his entire old age in Egypt. But Isaac was born in Canaan and died in Canaan; he never left Canaan. This is the Son, who was born in Canaan, raised up in Canaan, and died in Canaan. The Son is the One who "descended out of heaven, the Son of Man, who is in heaven" (John 3:13). He is "the only begotten Son, who is in the bosom of the Father" (1:18). When He was on earth, He expressed the Father, yet He never left the bosom of the Father. Hence, in typology, Isaac is the best figure of the Son.

According to typology, Isaac indeed typified the Son. But what kind of experiences did Isaac have? We can say that Isaac's experiences were all very common. Unlike Abraham, who did many things which had never been done before, Isaac only did what others had already accomplished. Abraham was truly the father, while Isaac was truly the son. In Genesis 21 Ishmael was mocking on the day Isaac was weaned, but we do not see any record of what Isaac did when he was young. When Abraham put the wood for the burnt offering on him, he did not say a word. When Abraham bound him and laid him on the altar upon the wood, he did not say anything either. He went wherever his father told him to go and did not say anything. At such a critical moment, he only said, "Where is the lamb for a burnt offering?" (22:7). In Genesis 23 his mother died, and in chapter twenty-four his father found a wife for him. He did not make any decisions, and he did not do anything for himself. He had nothing of his own. When he was sixty years old, he had two sons, which was not unusual, because Abraham also had two sons. God commanded Abraham to cast out the first son and put the second son on the altar, but He did not command Isaac to do this. Although God loved Jacob and hated Esau (Mal. 1:2-3), He did not ask Isaac to do anything. Abraham experienced a famine in Canaan, and Isaac also experienced a famine in Canaan (Gen. 12:10; 26:1). When the famine came, Abraham went down to Egypt. While he was there he told others that his wife was his sister. In the end he was rebuked by Pharaoh (12:18-19). Although Isaac did not go down to Egypt when the famine came, he went down to Gerar. He also said that his wife was his sister. In the end he was rebuked by Abimelech (26:9-10). Later, Isaac dug some wells, but the wells that he dug were those that his father had dug when he was alive. After his father died, the Philistines covered up the wells, and Isaac opened them up again. He called them by the same name that his father had called them (v. 18). After he died, he was buried in his father's grave. Even his grave was prepared by his father (49:30-31). This is the history of Isaac.

We have to learn the lesson of knowing God as the Son from these experiences. Not only do we have to know God as the Father, but we have to know Christ as the Son. What is the meaning of God as the Son? It means that everything is received and nothing is initiated by Him. In Abraham we see God's purpose. In Isaac we see God's power. In Abraham we see the standard which God requires of His people. In Isaac we see the life which enables God's people to reach that standard. Many Christians have one basic problem: They only see God's purpose but do not see God's provisions. They see God's standard but do not see God's life. They see God's demands, but do not see the power that meets these demands. This is why we have to consider Isaac as well as Abraham.

TWO THINGS IN ISAAC'S LIFE

We have to pay attention to two things in Isaac's life. The first is Isaac's relationship with Abraham, and the second is Isaac's relationship with God.

Isaac's Relationship with Abraham

Genesis 24:36 says, "And Sarah my master's wife bare a son to my master when she was old: and unto him hath he given all that he hath." This son was Isaac. *Isaac* means that we do not do anything ourselves or seek for anything ourselves. Isaac is the enjoyment of everything of Abraham. Everything is from the father. "Unto him hath he given all that he hath."

Read 25:5 again. "And Abraham gave all that he had unto Isaac." Isaac received nothing and acquired nothing through his own efforts. His prosperity had nothing to do with himself; it was from God. The Bible shows us that Isaac's characteristic was to inherit. Everything he had was from his father. He did not have to do anything. His father came to Canaan; he was born in Canaan. He did not have to worry about anything.

Isaac's Relationship with God

Isaac's relationship with Abraham was one of receiving. What was Isaac's relationship with God? Genesis 26:2-3 says, "And the Lord appeared unto him, and said, Go not down into Egypt; dwell in the land which I shall tell thee of. Sojourn in this land, and I will be with thee, and will bless thee; for unto thee, and unto thy seed, I will give all these countries." If we stopped here, we would think that God had established a direct relationship with Isaac and had made a covenant with him. But then God clearly said, "And I will perform the oath which I sware unto Abraham thy father." God did not bless Isaac because of himself, but because of his father Abraham. God's oath was given to Isaac's father. Now God was blessing Isaac as a confirmation of the covenant. Verse 4 says, "And I will make thy seed to multiply as the stars of heaven, and will give unto thy seed all these countries; and in thy seed shall all the nations of the earth be blessed." God had spoken these words to Abraham (22:17-18). He did not give anything new to Isaac. He gave to Isaac what He had already given to Abraham. How could all the nations of the earth be blessed? Genesis 26:5 says "Because that Abraham"; it was

not because of Isaac but because of Abraham. God says that
He is first the God of Abraham and then the God of Isaac.
Genesis 26:24 says, "And the Lord appeared unto him the
same night, and said, I am the God of Abraham thy father."
This is the relationship between God and Isaac. Then God
said, "Fear not, for I am with thee, and will bless thee, and
multiply thy seed for my servant Abraham's sake." God's
Word shows us clearly that Isaac's relationship with God was
based on Abraham's relationship with God. God blessed Isaac
because he was the son of Abraham. God was the God of
Abraham his father. Therefore, He blessed Isaac.

EVERYTHING WITH ISAAC BEING RECEIVED

From these two relationships, we can see Isaac's characteristics. Throughout his entire life, everything he had was a
matter of enjoyment and receiving. What does it mean to
know the God of Isaac? Knowing the God of Isaac means only
one thing: knowing God as the Supplier and that everything
comes from Him. If we want to know the Father, we have to
know the Son. In order to know the God of Abraham, we have
to know the God of Isaac. We are helpless if we only know the
God of Abraham because He dwells in unapproachable light
(1 Tim. 6:16). But thank the Lord that He is also the God of
Isaac. This means that everything that Abraham had was
Isaac's. It also means that everything comes by receiving.

If a Christian does not know the God of Isaac, he cannot go
on. If a Christian does not know the meaning of Isaac, he
cannot reach God's goal. In other words, if we do not know
how to receive, we will never reach God's goal. Those who do
not know Isaac can live only under Mount Sinai. Those who
do not know Isaac in life and do not express Isaac in living
possess nothing but the law. When God has a demand, they
try to *do* it according to themselves. When God wants something, they try to *offer* it according to themselves. This is not
Isaac. This kind of Christian eventually can only sigh and say,
"For I know that in me, that is, in my flesh, nothing good
dwells; for to will is present with me, but to work out the good
is not" (Rom. 7:18). The person in Romans 7 was willing to do
good; he was very desirous of being good. But he himself was

doing the work; he did not see that God must deliver him. He did not see that everything is in Christ, and he did not see the riches God has prepared in Christ. He did not see the inheritance in Isaac. He did not realize that the secret to victory is in receiving. He did not realize that Christians are Christians by virtue of who they *are;* they do not *act out* the Christian life. He did not see that God delivers a person by giving him the law of life. Therefore, he could only exercise his will.

OBTAINING VERSUS ATTAINING

The problem with God's children is that they realize God's demand on Abraham, but they do not see the way to meet this demand. After God's children see His goal, they think that they should do something to attain the goal. They do not realize that the Christian life, the overcoming life of freedom and sanctification, is obtained and not attained. The principle of Isaac is that everything is received. Salvation is something that the Lord Jesus has accomplished. Once we receive it, we are saved. Salvation does not involve a race to climb up the heavenly ladder, in which there is no assurance until one has struggled tortuously to the top rung. Salvation is not acquired in heaven; rather, God sends it to us from heaven. The same is true with victory. We do not have to strive for victory day after day. We do not overcome our sins by possessing an extraordinarily strong will. Just as salvation is received, victory is received. There is no need to do anything by ourselves; all that we have to do is receive. Once we see and receive, we can say, "Lord, I thank and praise You because I have received all in Christ!"

Second Peter 1:4 is a very precious verse: "Through which He has granted to us precious and exceedingly great promises that through these you might become partakers of the divine nature, having escaped the corruption which is in the world by lust." We do not know how many Christians have noticed the words "having escaped." How wonderful these words are! Many Christians say, "I wish I could escape." But God says, "Having escaped." He does not ask us to escape, nor did He say that He will work to the extent that we can escape.

He says, "Having escaped!" Having escaped means that the escaping is done. All that we have to do is receive. This is Isaac.

The meaning of Isaac is that God does the work and we receive the work. We do not crave, pursue, or hope over and over again. Rather, we sit down and reap the fruit. There is no need for us to worry about anything, because we are the sons and we are already "in." Since we are the sons, we are also the heirs and are qualified to inherit the possession of the family. Since we are Isaac, we can enjoy. This is all God's grace.

WORKING AND ENJOYING

However, what do many Christians do? They try to force themselves to do what they cannot do. There are things that they do not want to do, but they realize that God wants them to do these things. Therefore, they force themselves to do these things. Or they want to do something, and they know that God does not want them to do it. Therefore, they force themselves not to do it. They are Christians by their "doings"! This is absolutely wrong. This is not Isaac, because there is no enjoyment.

The proper way is to do things by the life that God has given us in Christ. This life spontaneously does what God wants us to do; it does not force us to do anything. At the same time, this life turns away from things that God does not want us to do. As a result, we do not have to force ourselves to turn away from certain things. We can turn away from them spontaneously. Whether we do certain things or do not do certain things, everything is spontaneous. There is no need to force ourselves to do anything. This is Isaac. God has a provision, and we should put ourselves under this provision. This is being an Isaac. When Abraham was about to offer up Isaac to God, Isaac only asked one question: "Where is the lamb for the burnt offering?" This was his only question. But his father answered, "God will provide himself." This is the characteristic of Isaac; his characteristic is to enjoy God's provision.

THREE SPECIFIC EXPERIENCES
A CHRISTIAN SHOULD PURSUE

What then is the meaning of the God of Isaac? The God of Isaac means that all of God's demands, expectations, and standards which He set forth in Abraham are fulfilled by God alone. In Abraham we see God's purpose, and in Isaac we see the operation of God's life. God's demands and standards are seen in Abraham, while God's provision and storehouse are found in Isaac.

The God of Abraham speaks of God setting up a standard for the vessel. The God of Isaac speaks of the fact that all the life and power one needs to become such a vessel and reach such a standard come from the Son of God. Isaac is the son, and the son inherits everything from the father. There is no need for a son to strive with his own strength. We will not reach God's goal just by knowing the God of Abraham. In order to reach God's goal, we have to learn to know the God of Isaac. But we cannot stop there. We also should know the God of Jacob. It is not enough just to have Abraham, and it is not enough just to add Isaac; Jacob must also be added.

Jacob was a crafty and deceitful person. Yet he met God. God's work in Isaac was a supplying work, while His work in Jacob was a smiting and disciplining work. These two kinds of work are different. God was always supplying Isaac, while He was always stripping Jacob. Isaac continually received grace before the Lord, while Jacob was continually chastised by the Lord. In other words, in Isaac we see God supplying Christ to us, while in Jacob we see the Holy Spirit disciplining us. Isaac shows us the meaning of the enjoyment of the overcoming life, while Jacob shows us the meaning of the dealing of the natural life. Isaac shows us the riches of the resurrection life of Christ which God has given to His children, while Jacob shows us how God deals with the natural life, the soulish life, and the fleshly energy until one day the root is cut off, and the hollow of the thigh is touched. God will not stop working on us until we realize that it is spiritually useless to do anything according to our planning, our wisdom, and our strength. God wants to teach us one deep lesson, which is to remove our self. In other words, the God of Jacob completes the God of Isaac, and the God of Jacob is for the God of Isaac. The life that God has given us is bound by our natural life and cannot be free. Therefore, God needs to deal with the natural life step by step. A Christian must be dealt with by God to the extent that others see a mortal blow in him. Unfortunately, some Christians have been dealt with by God tens and even hundreds of times, yet they have not received a mortal blow. Only a mortal blow will subdue Jacob and stop him from his scheming, planning, energy, and activity. Once the activity of the natural life ceases, the life that God gives us will be liberated. If we want to see everything that is in Christ being perfected in us, we must make sure that nothing in us comes from the natural life. We must cease from everything that is natural before Christ can be fully manifested in us.

What kinds of experiences should we Christians seek? We need a vision before God like Abraham had, we need a life like Isaac had, and we need the discipline of the Holy Spirit like Jacob had. These are the three specific experiences that we should pursue. We should never think that one of them is good enough. We must have all three experiences before we can become valuable in the eyes of the Lord. We must have a vision that sees what God is after. We must have a vision that sees that everything is of Him and that He is the Father. At the same time, we must know the life of Christ and know that His grace is our strength. If we live by the flesh, we will not reach God's goal. His work, not ours, will make us His vessel. After we have seen the life of Christ, we may still be ignorant of our flesh. Consequently, it is easy for us to replace the life of Christ with our natural strength and take the grace of the Lord to glorify ourselves and use it as our boast and our pride. This is why we need the discipline, like that which Jacob experienced.

When we have the vision, we see what God is doing. When we have the life, the overcoming life, we can praise and have the confidence to overcome. But there is still another aspect; God has to deal with us. If we know the God of Isaac, we will have the confidence to say, "But thanks be to God, who always leads us in triumph in the Christ" (2 Cor. 2:14). "Who shall separate us from the love of Christ?" (Rom. 8:35). However, we still need to know the God of Jacob. God's dealings with Jacob tell us that it is still possible for us to fail. We cannot guarantee our trustworthiness. If the Lord does not protect us, we can become weak and fallen at any time. In Isaac we know Christ. In Jacob we know ourselves. Because we know Christ, we have confidence, and because we know ourselves, we lose our own confidence. When these two combine together, we will fully live Christ.

Some people have seen that God is the Father, that He is everything, and that everything is of Him. Yet they still try to deal with themselves, suppress themselves, and restrict themselves by their own effort. While they are doing these things, there is nothing within them to positively support them. As a result, they go through much suffering only to find that they have not yet attained. This is not the spiritual way. Other people have seen that Christ is life. They have received Christ and the overcoming life. But they forget that their natural life still exists. They have not seen that their natural life needs to be dealt with just as their sins needed to be dealt with. As a result, they mistakenly regard things that pertain to the natural life as manifestations of the overcoming life. Again, this is not the spiritual way. It is not enough just to realize that Christ is the overcoming life. We must also see the natural life.

In order for us to be God's people, to be His vessel, to maintain His testimony, and to reach His goal, we have to know God as the God of Abraham, the God of Isaac, and the God of Jacob. All three experiences are necessary. Having just one or two is not enough. The day will come when God opens our eyes to see the vision of His demands. The day will come when God opens our eyes to see His work in Christ and that Christ is our life. The day will come when God opens our eyes to see that He has to touch our natural life and break its strength. If we see these three things, we will go forward. I repeat that these three things are specific experiences. Just as God revealed Himself to Abraham and became the God of Abraham, He has to reveal Himself to us to become our God. Just as He revealed Himself to Isaac and became the God of

Isaac, He has to reveal Himself to us to become our God. Just as He revealed Himself to Jacob and became the God of Jacob, He has to reveal Himself to us to become our God. We must know God in these three aspects. We have to know the meaning of God being the God of Abraham, the God of Isaac, and the God of Jacob. We must have these three experiences before we can go on in a proper way.

Chapter Eight

ISAAC IN THE NEW TESTAMENT—
GOD'S PROVISIONS IN CHRIST

Scripture Reading: Gal. 3:26-29; 4:6-7, 28, 31; 5:1; John 15:4a; Rom. 6:5-7, 11; Eph. 2:4-6; Gal. 2:20; Phil. 1:21a; 1 Cor. 1:30

THE INHERITANCE GOD HAS PREPARED IN CHRIST

We know that a man is saved by grace and not by the law. But this does not mean that grace is limited to our salvation. On the one hand, the book of Romans tells us that a sinner is saved by grace. On the other hand, the book of Galatians tells us that after a man is saved by grace, he should go on in grace. Romans tells us that a Christian begins by grace, while Galatians tells us that a Christian continues in grace. Galatians 3:3 says, "Having begun by the Spirit, are you now being perfected by the flesh?" Hence, a Christian should not depend on grace just for his beginning; he should depend on grace continually.

When a man is saved, he does not need to do anything by his own strength. All that he has to do is trust in God's grace. As he progresses, he still does not need to do anything by his own strength. Again, all that he has to do is trust in God's grace. This is the characteristic of Isaac. It is continuing in the grace of God. Not only is our beginning a matter of grace, but our continuation is also a matter of grace. From the beginning to the end, it is a matter of receiving. In the New Testament our Isaac is Christ. He is God's only begotten Son. He has become Isaac for us so that we can enjoy God's inheritance in Him.

Two Aspects of Grace

The Bible shows us that there are two aspects of the inheritance which God has given to us in Christ. On the one hand, we are in Christ. On the other hand, Christ is in us. In other words, there are two aspects of God's joining us to Christ. On the one hand, we are in Christ, and on the other hand, Christ is in us. We cannot confuse the order of these two unions. First we are in Christ, and then Christ is in us. This is why the Lord's Word says, "Abide in Me and I in you...He who abides in Me and I in him..." (John 15:4-5).

Our being in Christ has to do with the facts that are in Christ, while Christ being in us has to do with the life of Christ. In other words, our being in Christ touches Christ's work, while Christ being in us touches Christ's life. When we are in Christ, all the facts that are in Christ become ours. When Christ is in us, all the power that is in Christ becomes ours. When we are in Christ, everything that Christ has accomplished becomes ours. When Christ is in us, everything that Christ can accomplish becomes ours. When we are in Christ, we receive everything that Christ has accomplished. When Christ is in us, we receive everything that Christ is today. When we are in Christ, all the works that Christ accomplished in the past become ours. When Christ is in us, all that Christ is and can do today becomes ours.

We have to realize that all of God's provisions in Christ are our inheritance. If we want to understand the extent of God's inheritance for us and if we want to know the extent of the enjoyment of our inheritance, we must see that we are in Christ and that Christ is in us. Everyone who wants to know the Lord has to know Him in these two aspects. If we only know that we are in Christ, but do not know that Christ is in us, we will be weak and empty, and everything will be theoretical. We will fail again and again. However, if we only know that Christ is in us, without knowing that we are in Christ, we will suffer a great deal. We will find that we do not have the means to do what we want to do. No matter how hard we try, we will be left with imperfections. We have to realize that God's inheritance for us in Christ contains these two aspects. On the one hand, we are in Christ, and on the other hand, Christ is in us. These two aspects of our inheritance provide us with a rich enjoyment in the Lord. All the matters related to life and godliness, holiness and righteousness, and everything pertaining to this age and the next are included in the two phrases: "we in Christ" and "Christ in us." Both of these aspects of grace are a Christian's enjoyment. If we enjoy these aspects of grace, we will not need any self-effort. These two aspects of grace will deliver us from our own work. They will show us that everything is of God and that nothing is of ourselves.

We were sinners, and in order to go on, there was the need for a new start and a new stand. We were stuck in the mire. If we were left to ourselves, we would be in the mire forever. In order to give us a new standing, God pulled us out of the mire and set our feet on the rocks. Once we have a new standing, we have a new beginning, and we can go forward from there. We need to be delivered from sin, the mire, and we need to take a new standing. What kind of standing is this new standing? It is a standing before God. How can we be delivered from the mire, and how can we take this new standing? How can we come before God? We have the Adamic life in us, and we are wicked. We did not become wicked after we did something wrong; we were wicked as soon as we were born. Our conduct is wrong because we inherited a wrong life. When we first became Christians, we only saw that our conduct was wrong. After a long time, the cross did some work in us, and under God's dismantling work, we saw that not only was our conduct wrong, but our person was wrong as well. Not only is our conduct wrong, but the Adamic life within us is wrong. Our life is wrong; therefore, our conduct is wrong. This is what the book of Romans tells us. The first three chapters of Romans show us that our conduct is wrong, while chapters five through eight show us that our person is wrong. Since our person is wrong, what should we do? God's Word says that we should die. God requires that man's sins be washed away and the man who sins be put to death. "For he who has died is justified from sin" (6:7). Therefore, the only way to deal with the sinning man is to put him to death. But this is not all. In addition to death, we need a new life. When we die, everything is finished. If we want to have a new start before God, we need a new life. Therefore, we not only need to die, but we also need to resurrect. But we cannot stop at this point either.

Resurrection is not enough, and a new life is not enough. We still need a new position. Therefore, God transfers us out of the old position and puts us in a new position in heaven so that we can live before God. From this point on, we have a new position and have nothing more to do with the old position. Simply put, as sinners we have three great needs: death, resurrection, and ascension. With death, resurrection, and ascension, everything we have in Adam is terminated and we can have a new beginning.

We in Christ

How can we die, resurrect, and ascend? This is a big question, and it is a big problem. We cannot die, resurrect, or ascend. But praise the Lord that He has the way. He has joined us to Christ. Thank and praise Him. "But of Him you are in Christ Jesus" (1 Cor. 1:30). God has joined us to Christ Jesus. We have to remember this verse: "But of Him you are in Christ Jesus." This means that God's work has put us in Christ. God has put the believers into Christ Jesus. When God puts us into Christ Jesus, Christ's experiences become our experiences. This is like putting a photograph in a book. If someone takes this book and burns it, the photograph is burned as well. In the same way, God has put us into Christ. When Christ died, we also died. When Christ resurrected, we also resurrected. When Christ ascended, we also ascended. Our co-death, co-resurrection, and co-ascension with Christ are not something that we worked out, but something that God accomplished in Christ. God has taken Christ to the cross, resurrected Him, and brought Him to the heavens. Thank and praise the Lord. By putting us into Christ, God has made us partakers of the experiences of Christ. Since He died, we have died. Since He resurrected, we have resurrected. Since He ascended, we have ascended. If we look at ourselves apart from Christ, we have not died, resurrected, or ascended. But if we look at ourselves in Christ, we will say, "Hallelujah. I have died, I have resurrected, and I have ascended!" If we look at ourselves in Christ and believe in the word of 1 Corinthians 1:30, we will surely say, "Thank and praise the Lord. I have died, resurrected, and ascended!"

Because we are in Christ, all of His experiences have become ours. This is the first item of God's inheritance to us in Christ.

A brother once testified, "Over ten years ago, I had the following experience: I knew the doctrine of the cross, and I was able to preach this doctrine. I would not admit that I had absolutely no experience of the cross. Yet I realized that I had a problem before the Lord. There were many things in me that I could not say that I had dealt with. I did not have the assurance that I was dead to them. I knew about resurrection and ascension doctrinally. But I did not know these things experientially. For a period of four months, I sought the Lord and asked Him to show me the meaning of dying with Christ. I asked God to help me die with Him at any cost. I wanted to die with Christ at any cost. During those four months, the Lord showed me a little light, and I discovered one thing: God's Word does not say that I should be crucified. God's Word says I *have been* crucified. However, I could not believe this. When I looked at myself, I did not feel like I was crucified. I could only say that I was crucified if I was not honest with myself. If I was honest with myself, I could not say that I was crucified. I spent four months studying His Word and hoping to find the solution to my problem. One morning while I was praying, I suddenly saw that I was in Christ and that Christ and I were joined together. We two were one. I realized that it was impossible for me not to die when Christ had already died. This was something that happened within less than a minute's time. I asked myself, 'Has Christ died?' I could only say that Christ had died. I would be crazy to say that Christ had not died. Next I asked, 'What about me?' Immediately I jumped up and said, 'Hallelujah! I have died also!' I saw that since Christ had died, I had also died. My problem was solved. I am one with the Lord. Whatever God has done in Him, He has done in me. When He died, I died. When He resurrected, I resurrected. When He ascended, I ascended. From that day until now, I cannot deny this fact. This has become my inheritance." Brothers and sisters, this brother was speaking about God's inheritance to us in Christ. We should accept this inheritance.

Our being in Christ is an inheritance. All we have to do is receive and enjoy it. There is no need for us to do anything. However, many Christians go through many sufferings. They do not see that this is an inheritance and that this is something one receives and enjoys. They continue to suppress themselves and struggle to find their own way. Yet in spite of their repeated efforts, they find that they are still not dead and that their hopes have still not come to pass. Actually, the self that we cannot change and the old man that we have tried to shake off have been crucified on the cross by the Lord already! Because we are in Christ, we are crucified with Christ. Can we attain to this experience by ourselves, or is it something that God has given to us in Christ? This is the problem many Christians face. They think that crucifixion is an experience they have to attain to. But according to the Lord's Word, there is not such a thing. God has accomplished everything in Christ. All that we have to do is receive.

Of course, this depends on how much one has seen. Some have taken crucifixion as a doctrine, and they only understand it as a doctrine and teaching. This is fruitless. We need to have the revelation and the inward vision to see that we are in Christ before we can enjoy the fact of our crucifixion with Christ.

God has done everything in Christ. When we are in Christ, everything that is done in Christ is done in us. This is why 1 Corinthians 1:30 is so precious: "But of Him you are in Christ Jesus." Hallelujah. God has put us in Christ! Thank the Lord that He has given us not only Christ and the power of Christ, but even more the experience of Christ. Not only do we partake of the divine nature, but we partake of the nature of the Son of God, and we share in the experience of the Son of God. Of course, we are talking about His experience of death, resurrection, and ascension. We do not partake of His experiences before His death. At that time, the one grain was still one grain. But after the one grain died, His all became our all.

Christ in Us

However, the matter does not stop here. When we are in Christ, our past is terminated and we are ushered into the present, in which God has given us another part to our inheritance in Christ. This inheritance is "Christ in us." What is the purpose of Christ being in us? Christ in us is for the present and for the future. Christ is in us for the purpose of becoming our life today.

Many times we ask, "How can we overcome? How can we be righteous? How can we be holy?" We have to note carefully that God has not given us Christ as our pattern. He has not given us Christ as our power. God has given us Christ for only one purpose: "I am crucified with Christ; and it is no longer I who live, but it is Christ who lives in me; and the life which I now live in the flesh I live in faith, the faith in the Son of God, who loved me and gave Himself up for me" (Gal. 2:20).

The Means and Not the Goal

Many people are misled to think that God has made Galatians 2:20 our goal. After being a Christian for five or ten years, they hope that they can one day say that they are crucified with Christ and that it is no longer they who live, but Christ who is living within them. They think that this is the high goal toward which they should strive. Many people think, "I will keep pursuing, until the day I reach that goal. That will be wonderful." But Galatians 2:20 does not tell us that this is God's goal for us to achieve. It says that it is God's means, something that God has accomplished. This verse shows us the meaning of a Christian's life, and how a Christian should live out this life and satisfy God. Thank the Lord that we are crucified in Christ already. We do not need to seek to live with Him. Rather, Christ lives within us as our life. If we want to live out the Christian life and satisfy God's heart, the way is for us to no longer live, but for Christ to live in us. In other words, the Lord Jesus is living for us and on our behalf. This is why we can say that it is no longer we who live, but Christ who is living.

A Law

Paul said, "For to me, to live is Christ" (Phil. 1:21). This does not mean that Paul would reach a certain stage after being a Christian for many years and could then say, "For to

me, to live is Christ." He was telling us that this was the way
he had lived all along. What is the Christian life? The Christian life is just Christ. What does it mean for Christ to live
within us? Christ living within us means that Christ is our
life and that He is living instead of us. We do not live by the
power of Christ. Rather, Christ lives within us and on our
behalf. This is an inheritance that we can enjoy. God has
given Christ to us to be our life. A Christian life is one which
requires no self-effort, because the Christian life is a law. God
has given Christ to us to be our life. This life is a law, and it is
spontaneous. There is no need for us to do anything. The law
of the Spirit of life is in us (Rom. 8:2). We do not have to make
up our mind to do anything. When this law operates, it spontaneously does things for us. We need to realize that this life
is a law. If it were not a law, there would be the need for
self-effort, and we would have to do something. But since it is
a law, there is no need for self-effort, and there is no need for
us to do any work. Suppose we are holding something in our
hands. The minute we let go, the object will fall on the
ground. The force of gravity is a law, and this law will produce certain results automatically. Thank and praise the
Lord that the Christian life is a law and that we do not have
to grasp onto such a life. Thank the Lord that such a law
operates in a spontaneous way. God has put Christ in us and
given Him to us for our inheritance. He is working spontaneously in us. All we have to do is receive as Isaac did.

A Person

Let us read 1 Corinthians 1:30 again: "But of Him you
are in Christ Jesus." The first part of the verse speaks of
us being in Christ Jesus. The second part of the verse says,
"Who became wisdom to us from God: both righteousness and
sanctification and redemption." God has made Christ our
righteousness, our sanctification, and our redemption. Righteousness was originally a thing, but the righteousness that
God gives us is not a thing but a person. It is the Lord
Jesus within us becoming our righteousness. He is our righteousness. Sanctification was originally a condition, but the
sanctification that God gives us is not a condition but a

person. It is the Lord Jesus within us becoming our sanctification; He is our sanctification. Redemption was originally a hope, but the redemption that God gives us is not a hope but a person. It is Christ within us becoming our hope of glory.

Christ Himself

The daily life of a Christian is one of enjoying Christ and receiving Christ. On the one hand, we stand in Christ, realizing that all that Christ has accomplished is ours. On the other hand, while we live on this earth day by day Christ becomes everything that we need. Christ is the very things themselves. Our sanctification is just Christ, our righteousness is just Christ, our patience is just Christ, and our humility, meekness, and goodness are just Christ. Joy is not when we are happy. Joy is Christ living within us and being expressed as joy. Meekness is not a feigned appearance of weakness before others. It is Christ living within us and being expressed as meekness. Our joy, our meekness, etc., are all Christ Himself. These are the expressions of Christ.

This is what makes Christianity so special. We have a life within us, and this life is just Christ Himself. There is no need for us to use our own strength. This life will spontaneously express itself in meekness, goodness, humility, and patience. Christ in us becomes our meekness, our goodness, our humility, and our patience. We may think that meekness, goodness, humility, and patience are virtues that we possess, but God's Word shows us that these things are just Christ Himself. God has put His Son within us so that Christ Himself will live spontaneously out of us in all circumstances. When we are tempted by anxiety, this life will manifest itself as patience. When we are tempted by pride, this life will manifest itself as humility. When we are tempted by stubbornness, this life will manifest itself as meekness. When we are tempted by defilement, this life will manifest itself as holiness. Christ will express His patience, His humility, His meekness, and His holiness from within us. Christ becomes our patience, our humility, and our holiness. It is not a matter of our doing, but a matter of Christ living. We do not need to try to be humble by the power of the Lord; rather, Christ is our humility. We do not need to try to be holy by the power of the Lord; rather, Christ is our holiness. We do not need to fulfill God's goal by living by ourselves or even by the power of the Lord. The spontaneous manifestation of Christ Himself fulfills God's goal. When the Lord is expressed through us, we become what we are spontaneously. This is Christianity.

THE GOD OF ISAAC AND THE GOD OF JACOB

We have to know the God of Abraham. If we want to go on, we have to commit ourselves to the Almighty God and allow Him to reveal Himself to us as the Father at the proper time. We have to see that nothing from ourselves will satisfy His heart and that everything must be of Him, because only God is the Father. We must also know the God of Isaac. We have to see that everything is accomplished by Christ. In the past, He accomplished everything. In the future, He will still accomplish everything. His facts are ours, His life is ours, and His experiences and power are ours. It is one thing for us to be in Christ. It is another thing for Christ to be in us. Neither aspect requires any effort on our part. One day the Lord will open our eyes to see that everything is of Christ and from God and that everything has been accomplished by Christ. God is the source and Christ is the One who is working.

After we know the God of Isaac, we still must know the God of Jacob. What is the difference in spiritual significance between the God of Isaac and the God of Jacob? We can say that the God of Isaac shows us how God has dispensed His Son to us, while the God of Jacob shows us how God is disciplining us through the Holy Spirit. The God of Isaac shows us God's gift, while the God of Jacob shows us God's workmanship. The God of Isaac gives us the boldness to testify, "God has given me new light and shown me that Christ is my life. I have overcome!" The God of Jacob causes us to confess humbly, "God has shown me the self, and I can never trust in it again or boast of its usefulness." The God of Isaac causes us to proclaim boldly, "Sin is trampled under my feet!" The God of Jacob causes us to fearfully confess, "I can still fail at any time." The God of Isaac shows us Christ, while the God of Jacob shows us ourselves. The knowledge of the God of Isaac gives us the confidence to know that everything is done by Christ and not by ourselves. The knowledge of the God of Jacob causes us to know ourselves and delivers us from presumptuousness. If we study God's Word carefully, we will see these two different kinds of experiences.

We can say that the God of Jacob completes the work of the God of Isaac. The God of Jacob works in us to make room for the God of Isaac so that Christ will gain a place and occupy more and more ground in us. It is this very work that puts us "in weakness and in fear and in much trembling" (1 Cor. 2:3). Our life is a paradox. We have much assurance in Christ, and at the same time, we have no assurance in ourselves. On the one hand, we are bold to testify and speak, but on the other hand, we are fearful of speaking anything and feel like dust before Him. Without the blood of the Lord, we cannot face God. After we know the God of Isaac, we still have to go on to know the God of Jacob. When we combine these two experiences together, we have the proper Christian life.

CHAPTER NINE

JACOB'S NATURE AND
THE DISCIPLINE HE RECEIVED

Scripture Reading: Gen. 25:19-34; 27—30

Every careful reader of the Word of God cannot fail to find a great difference between the history of Isaac and the history of Jacob. Isaac's history was uneventful and peaceful, while Jacob's history was full of trials and troubles. Isaac's path was smooth, while Jacob's path was rugged. Everything that occurred in Isaac's life worked for him. Even when he encountered opposition, it was easily overcome. But most of Jacob's experiences were painful ones.

God is the God of Abraham, the God of Isaac, and the God of Jacob. Therefore, we cannot separate their histories. Spiritually speaking, the histories of these three reveal three aspects of a person's experience. God works on man from these three angles. Do not think that some people are absolutely like Jacob and that others are absolutely like Isaac. Thank the Lord that we are Isaac, and at the same time we are Jacob. On the one hand, we enjoy everything in the Lord. Everything is peaceful, rich, and victorious, and we can thank and praise Him continuously. On the other hand, the Holy Spirit continually works in us and disciplines us because of the presence of our natural life. God's Word says, "For what son is there whom the father does not discipline?" (Heb. 12:7). As sons, our Father receives us as well as disciplines us. Isaac shows that we are received by God's grace as sons, while Jacob shows that we are disciplined by Him as sons. On the one hand, God shows us that our life is like Isaac's; it is full and smooth, and everything that is in the Lord becomes ours. Everything that Abraham had belonged to Isaac. Everything that our Father has is ours. On the other hand, He leads us to partake of His holiness so that Christ may be formed in us and the Holy Spirit may bear fruit through us.

In reading the history of Jacob, it is very easy for us to stand aloof and judge Jacob as being unqualified for God's use and worthy of condemnation, especially if we have never been dealt with by the Lord and do not know our flesh. We find Abraham's history interesting, but we find Jacob's history irrelevant. However, if we are enlightened by God and realize what the natural life is and what fleshly energy is, we will spontaneously see that the aspect of Jacob is in us. We will realize that there is more than one aspect of Jacob inside of us. When we read the history of Jacob in his old age, we see that his seventeen years in Egypt were his richest years. In reading of his words, his deeds, his attitudes, and his acts, we cannot help but bow our heads and say, "God, Your grace can make a man like Jacob reach such a state!" When we come to the end of Jacob's history, we cannot help but exclaim in tears, "God, Your grace truly has turned a hopeless person into a useful vessel!"

Let us consider the way that God accomplished His work in Jacob—how God disciplined him, dealt with his natural life, and weakened him, how God caused Christ to be formed in him through the constitution of the Holy Spirit, and how he bore the fruit of the Holy Spirit.

What is the discipline of the Holy Spirit, and what is the constitution of the Holy Spirit? The discipline and constitution of the Holy Spirit are one work; they are not two separate works. We are constituted by the discipline of the Holy Spirit. We are molded by the carving work of the Holy Spirit. When our natural life is being dealt with, the nature of Christ is being constituted into us. While Jacob was being dealt with by God, he began to bear the fruit of peace. In the midst of discipline, the fruit of peace is borne. The fruit of peace does not come after the disciplining work. While God was touching his natural life, the fruit of peace was borne. This is the principle by which God manifested Himself through Jacob. On the one hand, we have to observe the way that God carved him and weakened him. On the other hand, we have to observe the way that God wrought the nature of Christ into him through the Holy Spirit. This work makes Christ's nature his nature.

The history of God's leading in the life of Jacob can be divided into four sections. The first section describes Jacob's nature (Gen. 25—27). It began with his birth and lasted until the time he received his father's blessing by cheating. This section tells us the kind of person Jacob was. The second section describes the discipline Jacob experienced (Gen. 28—30). It began from the time he left his home and lasted until Padan-aram. During this period, he suffered trials and discipline. The third section describes the dismantling of the natural life of Jacob (Gen. 31—35). It began from the time he left his father's-in-law house in Padan-aram, journeying through Peniel, Shechem, and Bethel, until he arrived in Hebron. During this period, Jacob's natural life was being touched by God. The fourth section describes Jacob's maturity (Gen. 37—49), that is, the period of his old age. It began from the time Joseph was sold to the time Jacob died.

JACOB'S NATURE

Let us begin with the first section of Jacob's history. What was Jacob's nature? What kind of person was he? We can learn about Jacob's nature from Genesis 25 through 27.

Struggling within His Mother's Womb

How was Jacob born? "And the children struggled together within her" (Gen. 25:22). This was Jacob. This was his nature. God's Word shows us that Jacob was totally different from Isaac. Isaac was an ordinary man. Everything with him came in the way of enjoyment; he inherited everything. But Jacob was a wicked and crafty person. He was calculating and clever; he could and would do anything. He had both shrewdness and ability. This was Jacob. But God was able to make Jacob His vessel to fulfill His goal. Isaac shows how one enjoys God's grace, while Jacob shows how one suffers under God's carving work.

God's Word shows that Jacob was not only wrong in the things he did; he was wrong in the kind of person he was. Not only did he dishonor God's name in the things that he did, but as a person he brought dishonor to God's name. He was a problem even when he was still in his mother's womb. He became a problem before his eyes saw the first glimpse of daylight. His wickedness began from his mother's womb. Rebekah prayed and asked God what was happening in her womb, and God said to her, "Two nations are in thy womb, and two manner of people shall be separated from thy bowels; and the one people shall be stronger than the other people; and the elder shall serve the younger" (v. 23). When Rebekah delivered, she indeed had twins. The first one to come out was Esau, and his brother came after him, holding Esau's heel. His name was therefore called Jacob, which means supplanter. Jacob did not want Esau to be great; he wished that Esau would have waited a little. Therefore, he took hold of Esau's heel. This was the kind of person Jacob was from the beginning.

In the eyes of man, Esau was an honest man. It was too much for Jacob to supplant his brother the way that he did. What can such a man be good for? This is Jacob from the natural point of view. However, from Romans 9, we find that the real issue between Esau and Jacob was God's selection. God said, "Jacob have I loved, but Esau have I hated" (v. 13). God had chosen Jacob to be His vessel.

Therefore, we have to learn to trust in God's selection. We have to learn to believe that God can bring us to perfection. God never gives up on anything halfway through. He is the Alpha, and He is the Omega; He is the beginning and the end. Since He has chosen and initiated, will He not complete His work? If God has chosen us, we have to learn to trust and commit ourselves into His hand. In God's good time, He will bring us to perfection. This was Jacob's case. God chose such a one as Jacob.

Many brothers and sisters have said, "I am a hard person to deal with!" Those who speak in this way need the God of Jacob. We may be hard to deal with, but if God could deal with Jacob, He can deal with us. Moreover, we have to realize that Jacob did not seek God; rather, God sought Jacob. While Jacob was still in his mother's womb, God selected him. Hence, if we know God's selection, we can put ourselves in

God's bosom; we can cast ourselves upon Him and trust that He will bring us to the point where we will be pleasing to Him.

Exchanging the Birthright
for a Pottage of Lentils

One day Esau came back from his hunting in the field and was fainting. He spoke to Jacob, saying, "Feed me, I pray thee, with that same red pottage." Jacob said, "Sell me this day thy birthright." At that time Esau was very tired and answered carelessly, "I am at the point to die: and what profit shall this birthright do to me?" As a result, Esau sold his birthright to Jacob (Gen. 25:29-34). This incident reveals the craftiness of Jacob's nature. Jacob treasured the birthright, which shows that he treasured God's promise. This is good, but it was not good for him to acquire the birthright through such a deception. This shows that Jacob was a person who used his own strength to gain what God wanted to give to him.

Receiving His Father's Blessing
through Deception

Jacob plotted with his mother to deceive his father. His father told Esau, "Go out to the field, and take me some venison; and make me savory meat, such as I love, and bring it to me, that I may eat; that my soul may bless thee before I die" (27:3-4). But Jacob, under his mother's guidance, took advantage of the weakness of his father's old age and feeble eyesight. He put on Esau's clothes, took skins of the kids of the goats, made savory meat, and received the blessing, thus deceiving his father (vv. 6-29). Once again this shows the craftiness and wickedness of Jacob's character. Some may ask, "If this blessing had gone to Esau, the elder would not have served the younger. Would that not have put God's promise in jeopardy? God's promise was to bless Jacob. By doing this, Jacob fulfilled God's promise. Was this not very good?" However, we have to know that God's promise does not require man's hand for its fulfillment. Will God's throne shake, and does it require man's hand to uphold and stabilize it? These are man's thoughts!

Jacob was a supplanter in his mother's womb. When he was young, he deceived his brother. Then he deceived his father with trickery. These incidents reveal Jacob's nature. He was very clever and crafty! This was Jacob's natural disposition. This was his natural life.

JACOB'S DISCIPLINE

God had to deal with a person like Jacob. After he received his blessing through deception, he could no longer remain at home. He knew that his brother would kill him, and he could only escape. He ran away like a refugee.

Away from Home

He cheated his brother out of the blessing. Yet in the end he received God's disciplining hand. The result of his fleshly activity was discipline. God exercises more discipline on those who are clever, capable, shrewd, and resourceful. However, we must thank the Lord because through His discipline, Jacob received the blessing. From this time on, God continued to discipline him so that he would be blessed through the discipline. He was forced to leave his father's house. He left his parents and set out on his lonely journey to Padan-aram.

Camping at Bethel

Genesis 28:10-11 says, "And Jacob went out from Beersheba, and went toward Haran. And he lighted upon a certain place, and tarried there all night, because the sun was set; and he took of the stones of that place, and put them for his pillows, and lay down in that place to sleep." He camped in the wilderness with stones for his pillows. His life of discipline had begun. Verses 12-14 say, "And he dreamed, and behold a ladder set up on the earth, and the top of it reached to heaven: and behold the angels of God ascending and descending on it. And, behold, the Lord stood above it, and said, I am the Lord God of Abraham thy father, and the God of Isaac: the land whereon thou liest, to thee will I give it, and to thy seed; and thy seed shall be as the dust of the earth; and thou shalt spread abroad to the west, and to the east, and to the north, and to the south: and in thee and in thy seed shall

all the families of the earth be blessed." These were the words
we read in Genesis 12. God now gave Jacob the promises He
gave to Abraham. When did God give these promises to
Jacob? He gave them while he was still supplanting and
before his fleshly and natural life was dealt with. God was
able to say these words to him because He was confident. He
knew that Jacob could not run away from His hand. One day
God would finish His work of making him a vessel for His
eternal plan. Our God is a confident God; He can reach His
goal. If a man were doing this, he surely would have worried.
Jacob was such an unreliable person. What would happen
if he became involved in some kind of trouble? But God had
absolute assurance. He was able to say, "In thy seed shall
all the families of the earth be blessed." God had decided. Our
hope lies in God's trustworthiness, not in our trustworthiness. Our usefulness depends on God's will, not on the
strength of our will. Brothers and sisters, we have to learn to
know Him as the God who never fails.

At Bethel Jacob heard God speaking to him in a dream.
God did not rebuke him. He did not say, "Look at yourself.
What have you done at home these days?" If it were us, we
would have rebuked Jacob. But God knew Jacob; He knew
that Jacob was a clever, crafty, and supplanting person. He
knew that Jacob had more energy than others and a stronger
disposition than others. Toward such a person, rebuke and
exhortation do not work well. God took Jacob into His hand.
Through operating in Jacob's environment, God chipped off
a corner here and a corner there; He carved a little here and a
little there. If He cannot finish His work in one year, He will
do it in two years. If He cannot finish it in ten years, He
will finish it in twenty years. God will always finish His
work. When God brought Jacob back to Bethel after twenty
years, he was changed.

God's promise to Jacob actually exceeded the promise He
gave to Abraham. It also exceeded the promise He gave to
Isaac. Jacob received something from the Lord that Abraham
and Isaac did not receive. God went on to tell Jacob, "And,
behold, I am with thee, and will keep thee in all places
whither thou goest, and will bring thee again into this land;

for I will not leave thee, until I have done that which I have spoken to thee of" (28:15). Hallelujah, praise the Lord! The promise that God gave to Jacob was unconditional. He did not say, "If you make Me your God, I will make you My people. If you keep My conditions and commandments, you will receive My promise." An unconditional promise means that God would always have a way to deal with Jacob whether he was good or bad, honest or cunning. God knew that one day He would fulfill "that which I have spoken to thee of." Our God is a God who cannot fail. We cannot stop God, and we cannot cause Him to stop halfway. If God has chosen us, He will definitely fulfill His promise in us.

Then Genesis 28:16-17 says, "And Jacob awaked out of his sleep, and he said, Surely the Lord is in this place; and I knew it not. And he was afraid, and said, How dreadful is this place! this is none other but the house of God, and this is the gate of heaven." He forgot about God's word to him. He did not think about the promise of the God of Abraham and the God of Isaac. He only became fearful because it was the gate of heaven. Bethel is indeed a dreadful place in the eyes of the fleshly man. We know that Bethel is the house of God. The house of God is indeed a dreadful place for those whose flesh has not been dealt with. In God's house there is authority and there is administration. In God's house, there is God's dispensation, glory, holiness, and righteousness. If the flesh is not dealt with, God's house is indeed a dreadful place.

"And Jacob rose up early in the morning, and took the stone that he had put for his pillows, and set it up for a pillar, and poured oil upon the top of it" (v. 18). This means that he sanctified the stone. "And he called the name of that place Bethel: but the name of that city was called Luz at the first" (v. 19). Then Jacob vowed, "If God will be with me, and will keep me in this way that I go, and will give me bread to eat, and raiment to put on, so that I come again to my father's house in peace; then shall the Lord be my God: and this stone, which I have set for a pillar, shall be God's house: and of all that thou shalt give me I will surely give the tenth unto thee" (vv. 20-22). This was Jacob's answer to God. This was the extent of Jacob's knowledge of God.

God said to him, "Behold, I am with thee," and Jacob said to God, "If God will be with me." God said, "[I] will keep thee in all places wither thou goest," and Jacob said, "If God...will keep me in this way that I go." This was Jacob's knowledge of God.

Let us consider Jacob's petition. His petition reveals the things he was after. He said, "If God will...give me bread to eat, and raiment to put on...." He cared about things related to his eating and clothing. He did not see God's plan. This word also shows us the type of discipline he had received from his parents. He was a spoiled child at home. He left his home only because of God's discipline. This was the first night that he had ever camped out, and he made the stones his pillows. From this point on, he did not know where his food and raiment would come from. Therefore, his mind was on food and raiment. He was disciplined in the matter of food and raiment. He saw that in trying to gain the blessing by guile, he ended up with no food and clothing, and he lost his father's house. Therefore, he said, "If God will be with me, and will keep me in this way that I go, and will give me bread to eat, and raiment to put on, so that I come again to my father's house in peace ... " His hope was to have food to eat and raiment to put on and to be able to return to his father's house. If God would do these things for him, he would do the following: "This stone, which I have set for a pillar, shall be God's house: and of all that thou shalt give me I will surely give the tenth unto thee." This was Jacob. This was the degree of Jacob's knowledge of God at the beginning. Whatever God would give to him, he would give back a tenth to God. His thoughts were very commercial. His communication with God was a kind of bargaining. If God would be with him, keep him, give him food and raiment, and guide him safely back to his father's house in peace, he would reward God with one tenth of his possessions.

This was the first time Jacob met God. Bethel was the place where God spoke to Jacob for the first time. Thereafter, when God spoke to Jacob, He always said, "I am the God of Bethel" (31:13). Although Jacob did not know God that well at this time, God left a deep impression in him at Bethel. This was the first time that God dealt with him. Twenty years later, after much discipline, he became a useful man.

The Discipline Jacob Experienced in Haran

Genesis 29 tells us that Jacob went to the land of the people of the east and saw the shepherds who came from Haran. "And while he yet spake with them, Rachel came with her father's sheep: for she kept them. And it came to pass, when Jacob saw Rachel the daughter of Laban his mother's brother, and the sheep of Laban his mother's brother, that Jacob went near, and rolled the stone from the well's mouth, and watered the flock of Laban his mother's brother. And Jacob kissed Rachel, and lifted up his voice, and wept" (vv. 9-11). When he met God on his way, he worried about food and raiment. When he had reached the land of the east and met his relatives, the first thing he did was weep. This weeping tells us what he experienced on his way and what he expected to face in the future. A scheming and calculating man usually does not weep. He weeps only when he finds that he cannot do anything anymore. Jacob wept at this point.

God was also ready to begin another work in him. When he arrived at his uncle Laban's house, his uncle said to him, "Surely thou art my bone and my flesh," and Jacob abode with him for a month (v. 14). After being a guest of his uncle for a month, his uncle said in a seemingly polite way, "Because thou art my brother, shouldest thou therefore serve me for nought? tell me, what shall thy wages be?" (v. 15). From this word we see that Laban's mind was also the mind of a businessman. He and Jacob turned out to be the same kind of person! When Esau was with Jacob, he could not deal with Jacob. But when Jacob met Laban, Jacob found it hard to deal with Laban. A quick-tempered person may often come across another quick-tempered person. A stingy person may often come across another stingy person. A proud person may often come across another proud person. A person who likes to take advantage of others may often come across another person who equally likes to take advantage of others. These are all thorny trials. This was what Jacob was faced with at that time. God's discipline put him before a man like

Laban. "Because thou art my brother, shouldest thou therefore serve me for nought? tell me, what shall thy wages be?" Apparently this word sounded nice. Actually, Laban was saying that Jacob should not eat his food for free, that he should work a little, and that he would be given a little money. Laban was only putting it in a nice way. In the past, Jacob was a son at home. Now he had to be a hired worker! This was God's discipline through the environment.

He served Laban, and the payment he wanted was Rachel. For Rachel's sake, he served Laban seven years. In the end he was cheated by Laban and was given Leah instead. Formerly he deceived others; now he was deceived! So he served Laban seven more years for the sake of Rachel. During those fourteen years, he served his uncle for the sake of Laban's two daughters. In all he served his uncle for twenty years. During this time, his uncle deceived him and changed his wages ten times. Originally it was agreed that he would get a certain sum of money after he finished his work. But after the work was finished, he was told that something was wrong, and his wages were changed. Laban changed Jacob's wages ten times. On the average, this was one change every two years. Jacob was indeed being tried.

But thank the Lord that this was God's hand upon him. In Bethel God said that He would bring him back to the land. God promised that he would return. Before that, however, He first wanted him to know God's house. God was holding Jacob. He put Jacob in the house of Laban, a man who was as crafty, clever, and shrewd as he was, so that Jacob would be dealt with. During this period, Jacob began to learn to submit under the mighty hand of God. But this does not mean that Jacob as a person had changed. Jacob still devised methods to make the lambs spotted and speckled so that they would become his. Jacob was still the same old Jacob. Even Laban could not deal with him. Even though Laban changed his wages ten times, Jacob still had the way to come out ahead of him.

God had a purpose in Jacob. In order to fulfill His purpose, God disciplined him in many ways. He wanted to deal with his strong points. This was God's work which He wanted to accomplish in Jacob. He dealt with Jacob step by step. For twenty years Jacob was repeatedly wounded and he repeatedly suffered. On the one hand, God was working in him to discipline him. On the other hand, his flesh was still present, and he was as cunning and crafty as before. However, God did not give up working on him. Through all of his adverse circumstances, he eventually came to acknowledge God's hand.

After Rachel gave birth to Joseph, Jacob thought about returning home. But his days of discipline were not yet fulfilled, and he still had to submit under the hand of Laban. He could not leave one day too soon.

We should believe that everything that passes through God's hand is good. Our circumstances are arranged by God and are there for our benefit. Every environmental arrangement is for our benefit; it deals with the strong points in our natural life. We hope that God will not need to use twenty years to deal with us. But unfortunately, some people do not learn the lesson even after twenty years. Although some people have been tested and disciplined, they never advance; it is a pity that their flesh is never touched or weakened, and they are still scheming and supplanting. Brothers and sisters, we should not complain that God's hand is too heavy. God knows what He is doing. Originally, Jacob was a merciless person, but after he was disciplined by God, he became a kind and loving person in his old age. May we see that all our experiences in our environments are measured one by one by the Holy Spirit according to our need. No experience comes to us by accident. All the experiences we encounter are arranged by the Holy Spirit and are there to edify us. While we are passing through these disciplines and trials, we may not feel joyful or comfortable, but they are all part of God's work in us. Afterwards, we will realize that these experiences were all for our benefit.

CHAPTER TEN

THE BREAKING
OF JACOB'S NATURAL LIFE

Scripture Reading: Gen. 31—35

There are a few meanings of the name *Jacob* in the original language. One meaning is "to grasp," and another is "to supplant." We have said previously that Jacob was constantly under God's discipline because of his craftiness. God would not allow him to be free. He made him leave his home. For twenty years, God allowed him to be cheated by his uncle in Padan-aram; his wages were changed ten times. This was a very difficult period for him. Jacob's experience was totally different from that of Isaac. Isaac's characteristic was one of receiving. It is quick and easy for us to receive riches from God. It takes only a short time for a Christian to enter into the riches of Christ and to realize that the facts in Christ and the life of Christ are his. The moment he sees this, he enters into it, and all problems are solved. But Jacob's experience was different; his experience lasted a lifetime. The natural life is something that lasts a lifetime. The activity of our flesh lasts for as long as we live on this earth. This means that we need God's continuous, long-term dealings; He has to deal with us step by step. We thank the Lord that this work will not be left unfinished; it will not be left undone. God will finish this work. God put His hand on Jacob's natural strength, and he became weak. Let us consider the third section of Jacob's history, which covers the way his natural life was broken through God's dealings.

PROGRESS

God used Jacob's years in the house of Laban to deal with him, to discipline him, and to subdue him. But Jacob was still

Jacob. No matter how shrewd Laban was, Jacob still came out on top. Although he was oppressed in many ways, he was still very resourceful; even his flock fell for his schemes. After twenty years, the time had come for God to speak to him. He had already had eleven sons, but this was the first time that God spoke to him since the time He spoke to him in the dream at Bethel.

God Releasing Jacob Back to Canaan

Genesis 31:3 says, "And the Lord said unto Jacob, Return unto the land of thy fathers, and to thy kindred; and I will be with thee." Verse 13 says, "I am the God of Bethel, where thou anointedst the pillar, and where thou vowedst a vow unto me: now arise, get thee out from this land, and return unto the land of thy kindred." God was calling Jacob to return to his own land. Subsequently, Jacob prepared to return to his kindred's land. Laban, however, did not want to let Jacob go. Although Jacob had somewhat taken advantage of Laban, God still blessed Laban for Jacob's sake. It was still better for Jacob to serve him than for him to shepherd the flock himself. Hence, Laban would not let Jacob go. After Jacob told Rachel and Leah of his intention and had their consent, he took his wives, children, and all the cattle and possessions he had acquired in Padan-aram and secretly left without telling Laban.

On the third day, Laban learned of this and went after Jacob. The night before he caught up with Jacob, God spoke to Laban in a dream: "Take heed that thou speak not to Jacob either good or bad" (v. 24). God would not allow Laban to say anything, because He was leading Jacob out of the place of trial and was taking him home. The time had come, and God wanted to release him. Every trial will last for only a limited period of time. When the goal of Jacob's trial was reached, God released him and Laban could do nothing to stop him. Laban heard God's word, and dared not say much when he caught up with Jacob. Eventually, they made a covenant. This covenant was very meaningful. "And Laban said to Jacob, Behold this heap, and behold this pillar, which I have cast betwixt me and thee; this heap be witness, and this pillar be witness, that I will not pass over this heap to thee, and that thou shalt not pass over this heap and this pillar unto me, for harm. The God of Abraham, and the God of Nahor..." (vv. 51-53a). Laban was the grandson of Nahor, who was Abraham's brother. Consequently, Laban said, "The God of Abraham, and the God of Nahor..." But God would not recognize this, so "Jacob sware by the fear of his father Isaac" (v. 53b). Laban could say politely, "The God of Abraham, and the God of Nahor," but Jacob could not say this. He could only swear by the God of his father Isaac. This means that the line of God's promise began from His choosing. God had chosen Jacob's father Isaac and his grandfather Abraham. God alone had done this, and no one else could interfere. Even Nahor could not interfere.

The incident following this was even more precious. "Then Jacob offered sacrifice upon the mount" (v. 54). Laban did not offer up any sacrifice; only Jacob offered up sacrifice. Jacob heard God's voice and began to draw near to God. He had made some progress. He went to Padan-aram because his mother had persuaded him to go; he did not go because of God's word. When he met God at Bethel, he did not do anything except make a vow to God. For his return God told him to go back, and he obeyed God's word to return. His relationship with God had improved. This was the first time he obeyed God's word. This was the first time he submitted to God and the first time he offered sacrifice to God. Although the twenty years of discipline did not make Jacob a different man, he now showed some desire for God. There was some progress. When Jacob took hold of his brother's heel and coveted the birthright and blessing, he was not after God, but after the goodness from God. In other words, he wanted God's gift and not the Giver. He wanted God's things and not God Himself. But after twenty years of discipline under God, there was some inclination toward God and some turn. Therefore, at the time of their covenanting, only Jacob offered sacrifice to God; Laban did not offer any sacrifice. After Jacob offered his sacrifice, he parted with Laban the next day and set out on his journey to Canaan.

Through Mahanaim

Genesis 32:1-2 says, "And Jacob went on his way, and the angels of God met him. And when Jacob saw them, he said, This is God's host: and he called the name of that place Mahanaim." The name *Mahanaim* means "two camps." This is a precious word. God was opening Jacob's eyes to see that as a result of his obedience to God to leave Padan-aram, God had delivered him from the hand of Laban and would deliver him from the hands of others. God opened his eyes to see that his company of people on earth was one camp, while God's army was another camp; hence, there were the "two camps." God opened his eyes to see that the messenger of God was with them. First, God came to him alone and said to him, "Return unto the land of thy fathers, and to thy kindred; and I will be with thee." While he was on his way, Laban came with a company of men, but God protected him. This proved to Jacob that God was with him. After Laban left, God gave him a vision and showed him that there was not only a camp on earth, but another camp of heavenly hosts following him. All of these incidents taught him to trust in God.

Scheming while Praying

Under such circumstances, however, Jacob was still Jacob. The flesh is still the flesh; it will never be reformed by God's grace. Although Jacob had seen the vision, it was a pity that he still exercised his maneuvering. Let us read verses 3 through 5: "And Jacob sent messengers before him to Esau his brother unto the land of Seir, the country of Edom. And he commanded them, saying, Thus shall ye speak unto my lord Esau; Thy servant Jacob saith thus, I have sojourned with Laban, and stayed there until now: and I have oxen, and asses, flocks, and menservants, and womenservants: and I have sent to tell my lord, that I may find grace in thy sight." This passage shows us that Jacob was a person who could resort to any amount of maneuvering and say any kind of despicable word. He would do anything to save himself from any disadvantage. He thought his words could change his brother's heart, but he had forgotten God's calling and protection. He had forgotten God's angels!

Verse 6 says, "And the messengers returned to Jacob, saying, We came to thy brother Esau, and also he cometh to meet thee, and four hundred men with him." Jacob was confused once again. He wondered if this word was out of good intention or evil intention. Esau was coming with four hundred men. What was his purpose? Verse 7 says, "Then Jacob was greatly afraid and distressed." This shows that those who plan the most also worry the most. The more anxiety a person has, the more fear he has. Jacob could only think; he could not trust. He could only scheme; he could not believe. He lived his days in fear and distress. This was Jacob. Those whose flesh is not dealt with can only trust in their own planning and scheming; they cannot trust in God or believe in Him. Therefore, they can only fear and worry.

Jacob's considerations were endless and his schemes unlimited. He was still making his own plans. He knew that God wanted him to return and that he could not stay in Mesopotamia any longer. He had to find a way to return. He could obey God, but he could not trust in God. He could not let God be responsible for the consequences of his obedience. He wondered what would happen if he encountered troubles as a result of obeying God. This is the experience of many Christians. They often obey God "at the front door," but at the same time prepare a way of escape "through the back door." Jacob was truly resourceful. He came up with an idea. "He divided the people that was with him, and the flocks, and herds, and the camels, into two bands" (v. 7). The "two bands" in this verse are the same as the name *Mahanaim* in the previous verse. Jacob divided his people and cattle into *Mahanaim*. He used this *Mahanaim* to replace that other *Mahanaim*. Originally, Jacob had one band on earth and God had one band in heaven, but now Jacob divided his band into two. He said, "If Esau come to the one company, and smite it, then the other company which is left shall escape" (v. 8). The goal of Jacob's scheme was to provide a way for escape.

Of course, he still knew something of God. Formerly, God had sought after him, now he sought after God. "And Jacob

said, O God of my father Abraham, and God of my father
Isaac, the Lord which saidst unto me, Return unto thy country, and to thy kindred, and I will deal well with thee: I am
not worthy of the least of all the mercies, and of all the truth,
which thou hast showed unto thy servant; for with my staff I
passed over this Jordan; and now I am become two bands.
Deliver me, I pray thee, from the hand of my brother, from
the hand of Esau: for I fear him, lest he will come and smite
me, and the mother with the children. And thou saidst, I will
surely do thee good, and make thy seed as the sand of the sea,
which cannot be numbered for multitude" (vv. 9-12). This was
Jacob's prayer. This prayer was not a high prayer, but we
must admit that it was much better than before. In the past
he only planned; there was no prayer. Now he both planned
and prayed. Jacob was planning on the one hand and praying
on the other hand. On the one hand, he was having his own
activity, and on the other hand, he was looking to God. Is
Jacob the only person who has done this kind of thing? Is this
not the condition of many Christians? Yet, in spite of this,
Jacob's condition had improved. His prayer and the position
he took were quite proper. He called God the "God of my
father Abraham, and God of my father Isaac." He knew that
God wanted him to return to his own land and to his kindred,
and that He would bless him. He told God plainly that he was
afraid his brother would come and kill him. He was honest,
and said to the Lord, "Thou saidst, I will surely...make thy
seed as the sand of the sea, which cannot be numbered for
multitude." He remembered God's promise and reminded God
of the promise.

At the same time, however, he could not trust in God. He
was afraid of what would happen if God's word failed. He
could not cast away his trust in God, because God had spoken
to him, but he considered it very risky to trust in God completely. He wanted to trust in God, yet without risk.
Therefore, he came up with his own ways. "He lodged there
that same night; and took of that which came to his hand a
present for Esau his brother; two hundred she goats and
twenty he goats, two hundred ewes and twenty rams, thirty
milch camels with their colts, forty kine and ten bulls, twenty

she asses and ten foals. And he delivered them into the hand of his servants, every drove by themselves; and said unto his servants, Pass over before me, and put a space betwixt drove and drove. And he commanded the foremost, saying, When Esau my brother meeteth thee, and asketh thee, saying, Whose art thou? and whither goest thou? and whose are these before thee? Then thou shalt say, They be thy servant Jacob's; it is a present sent unto my lord Esau: and, behold, also he is behind us. And so commanded he the second, and the third, and all that followed the droves, saying, On this manner shall ye speak unto Esau, when ye find him. And say ye moreover, Behold, thy servant Jacob is behind us. For he said, I will appease him with the present that goeth before me, and afterward I will see his face; peradventure he will accept of me. So went the present over before him; and himself lodged that night in the company" (vv. 13-21). This was Jacob's master plan! He was facing the peril of his lifetime; it was a moment of life and death. Jacob had passed through many things, but he had never encountered a situation as desperate as this one. He knew his brother's temperament, and he knew that his brother was a hunter who did not pity the animals. He was afraid that he would not have pity on men as well. This was Jacob's most perilous hour. He had never prayed as he then prayed, and he was never as fearful and as anxious as he was on that day. In Bethel God sought him out. Now he called on God. If you say that he did not fear God, you must remember that he prayed. But if you say that he trusted in God, you must remember that he came up with all these schemes and ways! He seemed to have forgotten God's promises, and at the same time, it appeared that he had not forgotten them completely. God delivered him out of the hand of Laban and showed him that a host of God's angels were going with him. However, he was still afraid and worried, and he was still planning and scheming. For twenty years God had subdued and disciplined Jacob, but twenty years later, Jacob was still Jacob. He was still very capable in himself. His eloquence was still with him, and he still had all kinds of schemes. Here he came up with his best plan. That night Jacob took his wives, children, and womenservants over the river first. Then he sent everything else over the river. He alone was left on this side.

THE EXPERIENCE OF PENIEL

God met him that night. "Jacob was left alone; and there wrestled a man with him until the breaking of the day. And when he saw that he prevailed not against him, he touched the hollow of his thigh; and the hollow of Jacob's thigh was out of joint, as he wrestled with him" (vv. 24-25). This place was called Peniel. It was the place where Jacob's fleshly life was exhausted and dealt with.

God Wrestling with Jacob

In this place Jacob was not doing something; he was not praying or wrestling with God. Rather, *God* came and wrestled with Jacob; God came and subdued him.

What does it mean to wrestle? Wrestling means to press someone down. God wrestled with Jacob in order to subdue him, strip him of his strength, and pin him down so that he could not struggle any longer. The meaning of wrestling is to deplete someone of his strength, bring him down, and pin him down. It means to subdue someone and then to keep him down with power. The Bible shows us that God wrestled with Jacob and *did not prevail* over him. Jacob was indeed strong!

What is the significance of God being unable to prevail over Jacob? When we do not trust in God and when we contrive by ourselves and are satisfied with ourselves, we have to admit that God cannot prevail over us. When we try to do God's will by our own strength and try to deliver ourselves by all kinds of natural means, we have to say that God has not prevailed over us. Many brothers and sisters have believed in the Lord for many years, but they have to admit that God has never prevailed over them. They are still very clever, strong, capable, and resourceful. God is not able to prevail over them. They have never been subdued by God and have never been defeated by Him. If they had been defeated by God, they would have said, "I cannot make it! God, I surrender!" It is unfortunate that many brothers and sisters have been under God's discipline repeatedly and still are not defeated. They think that they did not plan well enough the first time, and that they have to design a better plan the second or third time. Such ones have never been defeated by God.

Jacob was a person who would never suffer a defeat. He knew that this was a critical moment for him, but he still had his own ways. He might have thought, "I know Esau very well. If I do this, there is a ninety-nine percent chance that I will succeed." Although he was afraid in his heart, he was still very resourceful.

Many people have repeatedly experienced God's discipline, but their natural life has never been dealt with in a thorough way. As a result, they make God's discipline their boast in a natural way. They think that by experiencing God's discipline frequently, they are accumulating a rich spiritual history for themselves. If they had never been dealt with by the Lord, they would have nothing to say. They would not be able to take pride in any spiritual thing. The only thing they could take pride in would be the worldly things. But when they have had a little experience of fellowshipping with God and received some dealings, they adorn themselves with these fragmented dealings and use them as the basis for their spiritual boast and claim that they know God.

Brothers and sisters, perhaps God has been wrestling with you for five or ten years but has not yet prevailed over you. You have not yet been brought to the point where you say, "I am finished. I cannot stand up any longer. I cannot make it." This means that God has not yet prevailed over you.

God Touching the Hollow of Jacob's Thigh

Thank God that He has a way! It is true that Jacob was very capable and that his fleshly life and natural energy were stronger than anyone else's. But in the end God prevailed over him. If God had wrestled with him according to the usual way, the wrestling might have lasted for twenty years. But God knew that the time had come. When He saw that Jacob could not be put down, He touched the hollow of his thigh. Once God touched the hollow of his thigh, it came out of joint.

The sinew of the hollow of the thigh is the strongest sinew in the body. It represents the strongest part of a person, the seat of man's natural strength. God touched the seat of Jacob's natural strength.

God touched the hollow of Jacob's thigh because on that day, the sinew of it was revealed and exposed. On that day, he was afraid that Esau would come and kill him. He was afraid that his wives and children would be killed by his brother, and therefore, he put on the best performance of his life. He prepared his gifts, put some of each kind in each company, and asked the servants to walk in front and separate the companies by a distance. He also told them to speak good words when they met Esau. He came up with this smart way of mitigating Esau's animosity so that Esau would feel obliged to forgive. Jacob was putting his best ability forward; the sinew of the hollow of his thigh was exposed. But that day God touched the hollow of his thigh.

Man's natural strength always exhibits certain characteristics. There are always certain areas from which the natural strength manifests itself. There are always certain spots which are particularly strong. God intends to expose these strong spots. Unfortunately, many Christians do not know the vehicles upon which their natural energy is lodged. The most pitiful people are not those who are weak, but those who do not know that they are weak. The poorest people are not those who are wrong, but those who do not know that they are wrong. They are not only in error but in darkness. They do not live in the light. As a result they are not aware of their wrong. Some Christians can say that they are wrong in this and that, but the wrongs they mention are actually not the crux of the problem. There may be deeper problems which are not yet manifested, and God has not yet been provided the opportunity to expose them. God permitted Jacob to encounter Esau with the four hundred men so that all of Jacob's strength would be exposed and his characteristics revealed.

The Necessary Experience of a Christian

In order for a Christian to take God's way, he must receive everything from Christ. However, it is not enough for us to just be Isaacs. We are Isaacs, but at the same time we are also Jacobs. We need God to touch the hollow of our thigh, to weaken us, and to put us out of joint. The day will come when God will touch the hollow of our thigh. Our advance cannot always be slow. If we advance as slowly as we are now, it is questionable that we will reach Bethel in twenty years. God has been disciplining us for twenty years, but now we need to have the hollow of our thigh put out of joint so that we can no longer stand tall before the Lord. This is a specific experience, one that is as specific as our salvation. Just as we needed to be saved in a definite way, and just as our eyes needed to be opened to see the riches of Christ in a definite way, the seat of our strength also needs to be touched in a definite way so that our natural life will be dislodged.

Every Christian has his own thigh hollow. With some, their natural strength is lodged within their conniving. With others, their natural strength is lodged within their talent. Some Christians have their natural strength lodged in their emotions, while others have their natural strength lodged within their self-love. Every Christian has his own particular strong spot. His natural strength is lodged in that spot. Once that spot is touched, his natural strength is touched by God. I cannot tell you where your natural strength is lodged, but I can say that every Christian has his own particular spot. Every aspect of his life is under the influence of this spot, and this spot can be considered as the hollow of his thigh.

The natural life of some Christians is manifested in their love for exhibition. They love to exhibit what little spirituality they have. Their so-called "testimonies" are actually not testimonies for the Lord, but a kind of self-boasting and self-manifestation. All of their actions, life, and work issue from their desire to exhibit themselves. Eventually, God will touch their love for exhibition.

Some Christians have their natural strength lodged in their self-love. Everything that they do originates from their self-love. Those who are experienced can tell immediately that they are doing this and that and are saying this and that only because they love themselves. From all of their behavior, one can find a thigh hollow, which is their self-love. There is always a nerve center for our natural life within which strong power is hidden. Eventually, the Lord will have to destroy this before we can bear the fruit of the Holy Spirit. Otherwise, everything will still come from our self.

Some Christians have their natural life hidden behind their strong mentality. They always think and reason when others speak to them; they always judge whether or not something is rational or justifiable. They analyze everything that comes their way. Their minds are too active, and their heads are too big. They live in their mentality. If they do not think and analyze, they cannot live. Their mind becomes their life. They may be capable in doing many things, but they are useless in God's hand. Eventually, God will have to touch their mind before His purpose in them can be fulfilled.

Other things can also be the lodging place of our natural life. When God touches this spot, it means that He is working in us. This does not mean that we have become perfect, but it does signify a turning point in our life.

Many Christians seem to have committed unrelated mistakes. They make small mistakes here and there. The outward expressions of these mistakes may be different, but the root is the same. This root is the hollow of the thigh we mentioned earlier; it is the lodging ground of their natural life. God will not let this go; He will always come back to deal with it. God's attention is not on the many outward, minor expressions. His intention is to touch the nerve center of the natural life and to bring about a basic change in them.

Thank the Lord that He touched the hollow of Jacob's thigh. After this touch, Jacob became crippled. He became weak, was defeated, and could no longer wrestle.

The Meaning of Peniel

Some may ask, "What is the meaning of Peniel? How can Jacob's Peniel be applied to us?" We can answer this way: You may have a stubborn disposition which has been dominating your life. This disposition has become the principle of your life and the lodging ground of your natural life. At ordinary times, you do not notice it. But God provides many opportunities in which this natural strength is exposed once, twice, ten times, or even a hundred times. Yet you are still

unaware of it. One day, at the crossing at Jabbok, you will
have exhausted your ability and the very seat of your natural
life will be exposed. At that time, God's hand will touch
you and show you where your natural strength lies. You will
realize your most ugly, evil, and filthy disposition. What
you have been boasting about, what you have gloried in
and taken satisfaction in, and what you have considered
excellent and superior are now under the shining of God's
light and found to be nothing but the fleshly life, which is
filthy, corrupted, and despicable. The light has killed you.
This is the meaning of Peniel. God shows you that the very
things that you once boasted in, considered admirable, were
proud of, and that distinguished you from others are the very
expressions of the fleshly life. When God touches your life in
this way, you become weakened. This is the meaning of
Peniel.

Your natural strength needs to be dealt with by the Lord.
But before you see the light, you consider this strength as
something precious and worthy of boasting. Brothers and
sisters, you have to be careful with your boasting. The
strength of the natural life is hidden within the boasts of
many Christians. It is hard to find one Christian who does
not have his natural life lurking behind his boasts. Therefore,
you have to be particularly careful about your boasts. The
things that you boast in are often the very things that God
will deal with. Perhaps these very things are the hollow of
your thigh. God will shine on you and touch the hollow of your
thigh. When He touches this spot, you will become very
ashamed and say, "How could I have made my greatest shame
my glory?" All those who know a little about the experience of
Peniel can testify that when God touches the hollow of their
thigh, they are not only weakened but ashamed. They exclaim, "How could I have been so foolish? I thought that this
and that were good. Actually they were all shameful things!"
They feel that they are the most ugly person before the Lord.
Brothers and sisters, once God touches you, you will see that
everything you did before was ugly. You will wonder how you
could have considered them your glory and your virtues, and

how you could have considered others inferior to yourself!
When this happens, God has touched you.

The name *Peniel* means "the face of God" in the original
language. God's face is God's light. In the past, God touched
the hollow of Jacob's thigh with His hand. Today He is touching our natural life with His light. Once we are enlightened
by God's light, we will realize that the things we once considered to be good, glorious, and outstanding are but shameful
and foolish things. This light will give us a mortal blow and
deplete us of all strength.

Brothers and sisters, one day we will have to pass through
Peniel. God must touch our natural life before we can become
useful persons in His hand. The day will come when we will
pass through such an experience. Of course, we cannot hasten
its coming by being anxious. However, we can commit ourselves to the faithful Creator and pray that He will work
things out in the environment and lead us to the realization
that our boasts are just our shame and foolishness. May the
Lord be merciful to us, and may He give us light so that His
work may be fulfilled in us through the enlightening of
Peniel—the face of God.

No Pretense
in Dealing with the Natural Life

The natural life must be dealt with. Yet we cannot pretend.
Pretension is not Christianity. Christianity does not make us
persons we are not. If we are adults, we will spontaneously
have the appearance of adults. If we are children, we will
spontaneously have the appearance of children. The same is
true with God's work. It is He who touches our natural life
and removes its strength. As a result we cannot do anything
by ourselves any longer. We have to allow the Holy Spirit to
manifest Christ within us. We do not want to be natural, yet
we do not want to be pretentious either. It is an uncomely
sight for a child of God to pretend to be spiritual; it frustrates
his natural life from being dealt with. Many Christians
pretend to be humble. The more humble they appear, the
more uncomfortable they make others feel. With many Christians, it would be better for them to speak of worldly things

because they would at least be somewhat genuine. But the minute they talk about spiritual things, others cannot help but pray, "Lord, be merciful to him. He is talking about things that bear no reality at all." Many Christians appear very meek, but one cannot help but pray, "Lord, forgive this man's meekness; we do not know where this meekness comes from." Indeed, nothing frustrates the Christian life more than pretension. We have to be unpretentious and genuine. If we want to smile, we should smile. If we want to laugh, we should laugh. We must never perform and never pretend. The Lord deals with the natural life, and the Holy Spirit accomplishes this work. We must never exhort others to be what they are not. If a man is humble, he is humble. If he pretends to be humble, his pretension is worthless. If a Christian pretends to be spiritual, his natural life will become even harder to deal with. God does not need this kind of person, because his pretension is a frustration to God's work.

In the last century, there was a brother who was greatly used by the Lord. One day he was a guest at another person's house. A young sister was also invited as a guest. The sister was surprised to find that this brother was also a guest. She wondered if this brother would put butter on his bread. She thought that a spiritual person would surely be different from others. But to her disappointment, he did not fit her expectation of what a spiritual person should be. He appeared to be just a normal man! She was disappointed that he was merely a man! She observed that he buttered his bread just like everyone else and chatted while he ate. She did not see much difference in him. She wondered why such a spiritual man would be the same as others. She did not realize that his difference did not lie in eating unbuttered bread or in restraining himself from conversation at mealtime, but in his special knowledge of God. What was special about this man was his experience in the life of God.

We should never think that dealing with the natural life is pretending to be a special kind of person, one who is found neither in heaven nor on earth. We do not need to pretend or imitate. It is God who touches our natural life and God who deals with us. God touches the seat of our natural energy. He strips us of our own ways so that we can struggle no longer. Peniel is God's work; it is not something that we conjure up. The Lord wants us to be genuine. We should neither strive to become genuine nor "act" genuine. One sister appeared very genuine before others. But while she appeared to be "genuine," her heart was saying, "See! How genuine am I!" This kind of "genuineness" has no value before the Lord. She was faking her genuineness; it was a kind of self-boasting genuineness. We have to remember that the natural life is not touched when we pretend to be what we are not. God alone can deal with our natural life; we cannot do it. We need to be unpretentious. We should be what we are. God will deal with our natural life. Brothers and sisters, we have to be thoroughly clear that there is a big difference between anything that comes from ourselves and anything that comes from God. Anything that comes from God counts, while anything that comes from us is worthless. Anything that comes from ourselves only makes us someone we are not. Only that which comes from God will make us Israel.

A Sign—Lameness

Jacob was touched by God in the hollow of his thigh at Peniel, and his leg was crippled. Many Christians have this experience. But when they experience it, they do not know what it is. After a few months or a few years God may show them that He was dealing with their natural life. Then they will realize that they have passed through such an experience. Do not think that just because you are exuberant when you pray, your natural life has been dealt with by the Lord. It is wrong to think this way. Our experience tells us that we do not know when God deals with our natural life. But one thing we do know: Whenever we are touched by the Lord, we are no longer free in our walk; we are no longer as convenient as before. There is a big mark in us—lameness. Lameness is a sign that our natural life has been touched by God. It is not a matter of testifying in a certain meeting that God dealt with our natural life on a certain date. It is a matter of our legs becoming crippled through some spiritual experience.

Originally, the more we contrived, the more we enjoyed our contriving. But once we have been touched, something will vacillate within us when we contrive again. We can no longer contrive. The minute we try, we lose our peace. Originally, we were so capable of speaking about this and that kind of thing; we had lofty words and high sounding phrases. But even before the words come out of our mouth now, we feel sick about them. We can no longer be as glib as before. Originally we were shrewd and resourceful; we knew what to do about this person and what to do about that person. There was no need for us to trust in God. But after God has touched our natural life, we will feel that something within is gone when we try to supplant others; something within us wilts. We are not saying that we should not act wisely. God often will lead us to do wise things. But if we try to exercise our own maneuvering, we will feel that something has collapsed within us. We will feel this way before we even try to do anything. This means that the hollow of our thigh has been touched.

Those who have passed through God's dealings know the difference between natural strength and spiritual power. After a person's natural strength is fully stripped, he will be afraid of the resurgence of his natural strength whenever he works for the Lord. We know that we will obtain a certain kind of result if we say a certain word, but we are afraid of reaping that result. If we go on according to our natural strength, we will feel cold inside, and something within us will refuse to go along. This is the meaning of lameness.

There is also a difference in degree as to how much a person is touched by God. Some are touched by God just to the extent that their conscience is bothered. Some are touched by God in a thorough way; they are touched in the sinew of their thigh hollow. These people are the truly crippled ones. God has to do a thorough work in us until a life-long mark is left on us, a mark of lameness. After we become crippled, something will hurt us and frustrate us whenever we try to move or do something. This is the mark of being touched by God.

Jacob Laying Hold of God

Jacob's thigh hollow was put out of joint when he wrestled with God. But we see one amazing thing in verse 26: "And he said, Let me go, for the day breaketh. And he said, I will not let thee go, except thou bless me." According to our thought, Jacob's thigh hollow was already out of joint, and he was depleted of all strength. How could he not let God go? Yet the man said, "Let me go, for the day breaketh." This shows that when the hollow of our thigh is touched, we hold on to God the strongest. When we cannot make it, we turn and grasp hold of God. When we are weak, we become strong, and when we are crippled, we turn back to God and say, "I will not let You go." To us, it seems impossible that we can do this, but this is a fact. When our strength is gone, we find ourselves grasping hold of God. The grasping that happens when our strength is gone is the real grasping. Those who grasp hold of God have no need of their own strength. The faith that accomplishes things is the faith that is as small as a mustard seed. A faith as small as a mustard seed can move mountains (Matt. 17:20). Many times, fervent prayers and fervent faith are merely fervor; they do not bring about any result. But often, when we do not have the strength in ourselves to seek God, when we cannot even pray to Him or ask of Him, and when we cannot even believe, we find ourselves believing! The amazing thing is that this feeble faith, this little faith, brings in results. When Jacob was so strong, he was useless in the hand of the Lord. But when the hollow of his thigh was touched, God took hold of him.

He blessed Jacob saying, "Thy name shall be called no more Jacob, but Israel" (Gen. 32:28). The name *Israel* means "ruling with God" or "reigning with God." This was the turning point in Jacob's life. The experience at Peniel shows us that Jacob was defeated by God's hand; the sinew of his thigh's hollow was touched, and he became crippled for the rest of his life. Following this, however, God said, "As a prince hast thou power with God and with men, and hast prevailed." This is true victory. When we are defeated by God, we have truly prevailed and truly lost confidence in ourselves.

Whenever we find that we can no longer make it, that is the time when we have overcome.

Not Knowing God's Name

Let us read verse 29: "And Jacob asked him, and said, Tell me, I pray thee, thy name. And he said, Wherefore is it that thou dost ask after my name? And he blessed him there." Jacob wanted to know who the man was and what His name was. But the man would not give Jacob His name; He would only tell Jacob after he reached Bethel (35:10-11). Jacob did not know the man. He did not know when He came and when He left. Jacob only knew that his own name was to be changed to Israel; he did not know who that person was. All those whose thigh hollow has been touched by God are not too clear about what they have experienced. This is something that we must all realize.

After one brother heard the story of Jacob at Peniel, he said, "Last Friday night, God touched the hollow of my thigh, and He dealt with my natural strength." Another brother asked, "What happened?" The first one answered, "When God opened my eyes that day, I became finished. I was very happy and thanked the Lord greatly because He had touched the hollow of my thigh." It is questionable whether one can be so clear about his own experience. The story of Jacob shows us that when his natural life was touched, he was still not very clear about what had happened. If God has touched our natural life, we probably did not know about it at the time. We may only know about it after a few weeks or a few months. Some brothers do not know what happened to them when their natural life was touched. They only know that they dared not do something and were not as capable, strong, and clever as before. Formerly they had much confidence, but now their confidence is gone. Only when they turn to God's Word one day, do they realize that God has touched their natural life.

Therefore, we should not wait for such an experience to come. If our eyes are set on the experience, we may wait for a few years and still not get it. God does not allow our eyes to be set on our experience; He only allows us to set our eyes on

Him. Those who seek for experience will not find it, but those who look to God will find the experience. Many people are saved without being conscious of it. In the same way, many Christians have their natural life touched without realizing it. This was the experience of Jacob. He was not very clear at the beginning. He only knew that he met God that day. On that day, he came face to face with God.

Those who have passed through the experience of Peniel will not be able to tell others very clearly about the doctrine of it. All they know is that they have met God and that they have become crippled. They can only say that they are not as strong as they once were, and that they are not as confident as they once were. Every time they try to maneuver or contrive, they find themselves unable to do it any longer. Every time they try to prove their ability, they are stopped. Lameness is the proof of the thigh hollow being touched. One does not become crippled by shouting, "I am lame!" If a man still acts confidently, speaks persuasively, moves independently, insists on his proposals, and does not wait on God and look to Him when things happen, he is not crippled, and God has not touched him yet. Jacob did not know God's name; all he knew was that a mark was left on him, the mark of lameness. What does it mean to become lame? It means to no longer live by oneself, trust in oneself, or believe in oneself. One dares not consider himself clever or capable, and he dares not exercise his schemes. All he can do is look to God and trust in Him. He is in fear and trembling and remains in weakness. This is being crippled, and this is having the sinew of the thigh hollow touched. There is no need to spend time to consider when this will happen or how it will happen. All we have to do is look to the Lord and believe that one day, subconsciously the sinew of our thigh hollow will be touched.

However, the experience of Peniel alone is not complete. Peniel signifies God's beginning. It was there that God first told Jacob that he would be called Israel. After Peniel it is hard for us to detect Israel in Jacob. We still see Jacob. In Peniel Jacob only knew that his own name would be called Israel; he did not know God's name. Jacob did not know who God was until Genesis 35. Hence, Peniel was only a turning point. The completion is not found until we come to Bethel. More time was needed before God's work could be completed in Jacob.

THE CONTINUATION OF THE OLD BEHAVIOR

Jacob became crippled after Peniel, but he still did not know what he had experienced. When the day broke, he still acted according to his original plan.

Many people condemn Jacob and pass judgment on him. They think that Jacob should have stopped his activities because he had been touched by God. Since he was touched by God already, every problem should have been solved. This is the mentality of those who do not know themselves. They think that everything is clear-cut and that all of their problems can be solved in one breath. Actually, things are never that simple. We have to realize that experience is not a whim of an idea. Jacob could not become Israel in an instant. Since he had made all the arrangements the day before, he carried out his scheme as planned. But we have to realize one thing: After God touched the hollow of his thigh, he was different when he met Esau. We can see that Jacob was beginning to change.

Let us read Genesis 33:1-3: "And Jacob lifted up his eyes, and looked, and, behold, Esau came, and with him four hundred men. And he divided the children unto Leah, and unto Rachel, and unto the two handmaids. And he put the handmaids and their children foremost, and Leah and her children after, and Rachel and Joseph hindermost. And he passed over before them, and bowed himself to the ground seven times, until he came near to his brother." He was still as cunning as before. He even bowed down seven times to the ground before his brother. Verse 4 says, "And Esau ran to meet him, and embraced him, and fell on his neck, and kissed him: and they wept." Jacob did not expect that his schemes would not be needed and that all his plans were in vain. God's protection was real. All he needed was a little faith and he could have avoided much vexation and fear! Esau did not try to kill him; rather, he was coming to welcome him. He embraced Jacob, fell on his neck, and kissed him. All of Jacob's cleverness and plans came to nothing! When he left his brother and met Rachel, he wept. Now when he came back and met Esau, he wept again. Some people weep because they like to weep by nature. But Jacob was a resourceful person; he did not weep easily. However, when he saw his brother, he wept. This was a rare occasion. This means that the experience of Peniel had made Jacob a soft person.

Verses 6 through 8 say, "Then the handmaidens came near, they and their children, and they bowed themselves. And Leah also with her children came near, and bowed themselves: and after came Joseph near and Rachel, and they bowed themselves. And he said, What meanest thou by all this drove which I met? And he said, These are to find grace in the sight of my lord." He was still delivering the speech he had prepared the day before. The day before he had prepared to call Esau "my lord." He went according to the original plan and called him "my lord." A man can be dealt with in his natural life, and his power can be stripped by God, but his outward conduct may take a few weeks or even a few months to change.

Verses 9 and 10 say, "And Esau said, I have enough, my brother; keep that thou hast unto thyself. And Jacob said, Nay, I pray thee, if now I have found grace in thy sight, then receive my present at my hand: for therefore I have seen thy face, as though I had seen the face of God, and thou wast pleased with me." We should not consider this word as Jacob's pretense. He said, "I have seen thy face, as though I had seen the face of God." Jacob was not trying to be humble in saying this. Of course Jacob was very good at pretending, but this word was not his pretense. There was deep significance to his word. This word means that for him to see Esau's face was for him to face Peniel. What does this mean? It means that when one sees the face of those he has offended and sinned against, he sees the face of God. Whenever we meet those whom we have sinned against, we meet God. Whenever we come across those whom we have offended, we come across judgment. If we owe anyone anything, if we have ill-treated anyone, or if we have done anyone harm, we will see God every time we see them if the matter is not settled. They will become as fearful as God. Every time we see their face we will be reminded of God, and every time we come across their way we will come across judgment. Jacob was stating the real fact. For Jacob, seeing Esau's face was indeed "as though I had seen the face of God."

BACK TO CANAAN

Esau returned to Seir, and Jacob set off to Succoth. "And Jacob came to Shalem, a city of Shechem, which is in the land of Canaan, when he came from Padan-aram; and pitched his tent before the city" (v. 18).

Remaining in Shechem

God wanted Jacob to go back to his father's land, but he remained in Shechem. Shechem was only the first stop on the way to Canaan, yet Jacob dwelt in Shechem. First, he built a house in Succoth (v. 17). Then he bought a parcel of a field, spread his tent, and erected an altar in Shechem, and called it "El-Elohe-Israel," which means "God, the God of Israel" (vv. 19-20). He had not reached Bethel nor Hebron yet; he was only in Shechem, and he dwelt there. He not only dwelt there, but he bought a piece of land there. This shows that Jacob was not strong enough and had not learned the lesson properly. He had not reached the state of perfection. God's dealing with Jacob was gradual. The discipline of God and the constitution of the Holy Spirit were carried out step by step.

Although it was a failure for Jacob to remain in Shechem, he nevertheless built an altar there, called on the name of God, and proclaimed God to be the God of Israel. This was a progression. God was now not only the God of Abraham and the God of Isaac, but "El-Elohe-Israel." "El" is God, and "Elohe" is also God. The meaning of the whole word is "The God of Israel is indeed God," or "God is indeed the God of Israel." He could now say such a word. He had indeed made some progress before the Lord.

In chapter thirty-four, Jacob's daughter was defiled in that land, and two of his sons plotted and killed Shechem and all the males of the city. This put Jacob in a very difficult situation. It was then that God called him to Bethel (35:1). God disciplined him and guided him. He wanted to live in Shechem, but God would not let him live there for too long.

We have mentioned before that Abraham lived in three places in Canaan: Shechem, Bethel, and Hebron. He built altars in all three places. These three places carry the characteristics of Canaan; they are in fact a representation of the land of Canaan. After Peniel, God intended to take Jacob on the path of Abraham, first to Shechem, then to Bethel, and finally to Hebron. Abraham passed through these three places, and God led Jacob through these three places as well. After Peniel, God led him on to Shechem and then to Bethel. Peniel and Bethel match one another. At Peniel God said, "Thy name shall be called no more Jacob, but Israel" (32:28), and at Bethel He also said, "Thy name is Jacob: thy name shall not be called any more Jacob" (35:10). In other words, Peniel was the beginning, while Bethel was the completion.

Going to Bethel

Genesis 35:1 says, "And God said unto Jacob, Arise, go up to Bethel, and dwell there: and make there an altar unto God, that appeared unto thee when thou fleddest from the face of Esau thy brother." God told him to go up to Bethel. Bethel was a place that particularly touched Jacob's heart because he dreamed and God appeared to him there. We have mentioned earlier that Bethel means the house of God; it signifies the authority of Christ, that Christ is ruling over His house. It also signifies the corporate life, which is the Body of Christ. In this house there should not be any defilement, sin, or anything that is contrary to God's will. This is why Jacob told his household and those who were with him to "put away the strange gods that are among you, and be clean, and change your garments" when they went up to Bethel (v. 2). In other words, they had to leave behind everything that was related to the idols before they could go up to Bethel. In Shechem Jacob buried the strange gods and all their earrings under the oak (v. 4). The meaning of *Shechem* is "strength of the shoulder." In other words, Christ deals with our idols and our sins, and Christ deals with all the things which we cannot deal with. The oak of Shechem speaks of the riches of Isaac; it shows us that everything contrary to us is dealt with there. In Shechem Christ has enough power to deal with all these things. His shoulder is broad enough to bear all these responsibilities. Bethel is the house of God. There should only be clean conduct and clean living in the house of God, and all the unclean things should be dealt with before one can go up to Bethel. God demands not only that we have a clean living individually, but that we also have a clean living corporately. Bethel cannot tolerate any unclean things. The Body of Christ is Christ, and only Christ can remain in His Body; everything else must be left behind in Shechem.

Verse 5 says, "And they journeyed." After Jacob trusted in the power of the Lord and removed all the things that did not glorify Him, he set out on his journey.

Verses 6 and 7 say, "So Jacob came to Luz which is in the land of Canaan, that is, Bethel, he and all the people that were with him. And he built there an altar, and called the place El-bethel; because there God appeared unto him, when he fled from the face of his brother." At that time, Jacob took another step forward. In Shechem he called the place "El-Elohe-Israel." Here he called it "El-bethel." In Shechem he called God the God of Israel, while here he called God the God of Bethel. He advanced from the individual experience to the corporate experience. In Shechem he knew God as the God of Israel. When he reached Bethel, he knew God as the God of His house. When he reached Bethel, he realized that the vessel God is after is a house, a corporate vessel. God was not only his God, but the God of His house. He was brought to a broadened place.

Thank and praise the Lord that God is not heaping up piles of isolated stones; He is building a house that expresses Him. There must be the corporate testimony before God's goal can be reached. Individuals cannot satisfy God's heart. Even many individuals working for the Lord will not satisfy God's heart. There is the need of a corporate vessel to fulfill God's purpose and satisfy His heart. Our God is the God of Bethel, the God of the church.

Here God appeared to Jacob once more. This appearance of God in Bethel was different from His previous appearance in Bethel. The previous time God had appeared in a dream. This time He appeared directly. Let us read verses 9 and 10: "And God appeared unto Jacob again, when he came out of Padan-aram, and blessed him. And God said unto him, Thy name is Jacob: thy name shall not be called any more Jacob, but Israel shall be thy name; and he called his name Israel." At Peniel God began to change his name from Jacob to Israel. At Bethel the changing of his name was actually carried out. What began at Peniel was completed in the house of God. At Peniel God dealt with Jacob's natural life. God worked in him and gave him a mortal blow. After Peniel only a mere vestige of his natural life remained; it was no longer as strong as it once was. When he reached Bethel, that which began with his enlightening at Peniel was perfected in the house of God. Having our natural life touched individually is the starting point of Israel, while knowing the Body of Christ in the house of God is the perfection of Israel. The beginning of the experience of Peniel is the enlightening and the stripping of the natural life, while the completion of the experience of Peniel is Bethel, the house of God.

God said to Jacob, "I am God Almighty" (v. 11). Jacob heard what he did not hear at Peniel. At Peniel Jacob asked God for His name, and God would not tell him. God told him His name here. "I am God Almighty!" This was one of the names God revealed to Abraham when He appeared to him (17:1). God said this to Jacob to show him not only his own impotence, but God's omnipotence. Not only do we have to know our poverty, but we have to know His riches. "Be fruitful and multiply; a nation and a company of nations shall be of thee, and kings shall come out of thy loins; and the land which I gave Abraham and Isaac, to thee I will give it, and to thy seed after thee will I give the land" (35:11-12). This shows that God had secured a new vessel in Jacob. Now there was a people who could fulfill God's purpose on earth. After God spoke this, He went up from him (v. 13). When Jacob met God previously, he erected a stone to be a pillar, poured oil on it, and called the name of the place the house of God. At that time, he was afraid and felt that the place was very dreadful. After Jacob met God this time, he set up a pillar of stone and poured oil as well as a drink offering on it (v. 14). A drink offering is an offering of wine; in the Bible it signifies joy. Now Jacob was no longer fearful but joyful. Previously, he felt dreadful when he met God. Now he was joyful when he met God. This shows us that when we are saved, there is a certain taste in our praise of the Lord, and when our flesh is dealt with, there is another taste in our praise of the Lord. The taste of praise which comes after the flesh is dealt with is something which one can never experience prior to being dealt with.

Dwelling in Hebron

Verse 16 says, "And they journeyed from Bethel." Verse 27 says, "And Jacob came unto Isaac his father unto Mamre, unto the city of Arba, which is Hebron, where Abraham and Isaac sojourned." Jacob had arrived in Hebron. Once he reached this place, God's work in him was completed. From this point on, he dwelt in Hebron, the place where Abraham and Isaac once dwelt. The meaning of Hebron is to remain in the fellowship. It was not only fellowship with God but fellowship with the other members of the Body of Christ.

Bethel was not the permanent dwelling place for Jacob. Only Hebron was the permanent dwelling place of Abraham, Isaac, and Jacob. This means that we need to know Bethel as the house of God just as we need to know Shechem as the power of God. However, we do not live in the knowledge of the house of God; we live daily in the fellowship of it.

From that time on, Jacob realized that he could do nothing on his own. Everything had to be done in fellowship, and nothing could be done outside of fellowship. If the flesh is not dealt with, it will never see the importance of fellowship. Many Christians do not seem to need fellowship. They do not need to fellowship with God, and they do not need to fellowship with other children of God. They are this way mainly because their flesh has never been dealt with. The flesh must be dealt with, and one must know the life of Bethel before he realizes that he cannot live outside Hebron, and that he cannot survive without fellowship. The fellowship we are speaking of refers to the life supply of Christ which comes from the other members. When other brothers and sisters supply us with the indwelling Christ and we go forward through the supply of these other members, we have Hebron and fellowship. God's children are very much in need of this.

If God's children have not been dealt with in their flesh, they cannot know the life of the Body of Christ. They may understand the doctrine about the Body of Christ, and they may even be able to expound it clearly. But if their flesh is not dealt with, they will not know the life of the Body. Once the flesh is dealt with, they will know the life of the Body of Christ. They will see the importance of fellowship, and they will not be able to live apart from the fellowship. They will not be able to be a Christian at all without the other children of God, and they will not be able to receive any supply of life apart from the help of God's children. Brothers and sisters, the Body of Christ is a fact; it is not a doctrine. We cannot live without Christ, and we cannot live without the other Christians.

We have to ask God to show us that we cannot be Christians by ourselves. We have to live in fellowship with God, and we have to live in fellowship with the Body of Christ. May God lead us on so that we can truly glorify His name. May God gain not only a vessel in Jacob, but a vessel in us as well.

CHAPTER ELEVEN

THE MATURITY OF JACOB

Scripture Reading: Gen. 37; 42—49

After Jacob was dealt with by God at Peniel, he began to recognize his own weakness and was gradually changed. He gradually saw the way he should take; he passed through Shechem to Bethel and finally dwelt in Hebron. However, this does not mean that Jacob needed no further dealings from God after Peniel. The Bible shows us that after Peniel, he seemed to encounter even more dealings from God than before. We may say that Jacob was a suffering-ridden person. From Shechem to Bethel and from Bethel to Hebron, Jacob suffered many sorrows. We can take a look at the following examples.

In Shechem Jacob met a very difficult situation. His daughter was defiled by Shechem, the son of Hamor the Hivite, the prince of the country. Jacob's sons then conspired to slay Shechem and all the males in the city. This matter greatly troubled Jacob. Let us read Genesis 34:30: "And Jacob said to Simeon and Levi, Ye have troubled me to make me to stink among the inhabitants of the land, among the Canaanites and the Perizzites: and I being few in number, they shall gather themselves together against me, and slay me; and I shall be destroyed, I and my house." Jacob was very worried that Shechem's countrymen might rise up in revenge to destroy him and his entire house. This was the crisis that confronted Jacob in Shechem.

In chapter thirty-five Jacob went to Bethel and encountered another incident. "Deborah Rebekah's nurse died" (v. 8). He could not see his mother, but if his mother's nurse was there, he would have been somewhat comforted. He did not expect that his mother's nurse would die also. The Scripture purposely records that "she was buried beneath Bethel under an oak: and the name of it was called Allon-bachuth." The meaning of *Allon-bachuth* in the original language is "the oak of weeping." From this we have a glimpse of Jacob's sorrow and grief at that time.

He journeyed from Bethel, and when he was close to Ephrath, he was met with an even more sorrowful event. "Rachel travailed, and she had hard labor....And it came to pass, as her soul was in departing, (for she died,) that she called his name Benoni: but his father called him Benjamin. And Rachel died, and was buried in the way to Ephrath, which is Bethlehem. And Jacob set a pillar upon her grave: that is the pillar of Rachel's grave unto this day" (vv. 16-20). The wife whom Jacob loved so much died on the way. The pillar that he set upon Rachel's grave told of his sad story.

When Jacob was in Edar, he experienced another heart-breaking thing. His son Reuben went to lay with Bilhah, Jacob's concubine (v. 22). This was another matter that caused Jacob to suffer.

After he passed through all these incidents, he arrived at Hebron where his father Isaac sojourned. Here the Bible makes no mention of his mother Rebekah; perhaps his mother had already died. This was God's severe dealing with Jacob. In his youth his mother had loved him. His mother had taught him how to steal the blessing that his brother Esau should have received. But now the mother who had loved him so dearly was no longer around. He truly experienced many sorrows.

At this point we have completed our study of the third stage of Jacob's history. In the first stage of his history, we saw his disposition. In the second stage of his history, we saw the trials and disciplines that he suffered. In the third stage of his history, we saw that God not only disciplined him, but also dealt with his being and his natural life. Even after his natural life had been thoroughly dealt with, we see that the discipline of God was still upon him. God dealt with him in this way for the purpose of creating in him a character that he did not possess before.

The section from chapter thirty-seven to the end of Jacob's old age may be considered the fourth stage of Jacob's history. We may also say that this was the period of the maturing of Jacob, the brightest period in Jacob's entire life. Proverbs 4:18 says, "But the path of the just is as the shining light, that shineth more and more unto the perfect day." Jacob shone brighter day by day until his death. During this period of almost forty years, Jacob did not do much, yet before God he was transformed fully into a man of grace and love.

We can see from the Bible that a Christian need not regress and decline in his old age. The three top apostles in the New Testament all shone brightly at the time of their death. When Peter wrote his second Epistle, it was close to the time of his departure from his tabernacle. But he still reminded and exhorted the brothers while he was yet in his tabernacle. In particular he said that he was an eyewitness of the Lord's glory and power. There was absolutely no waning of the brightness of Peter's shining. As for Paul, he said, "For I am already being poured out, and the time of my departure is at hand....Henceforth there is laid up for me the crown of righteousness, with which the Lord, the righteous Judge, will recompense me in that day" (2 Tim. 4:6-8). We can see from these sentences that the hope he had toward the Lord was brightly shining. With the apostle John, who wrote his Gospel, his Epistles, and the book of Revelation during his old age, this shining is most apparent. The Gospel he wrote says, "In the beginning was the Word." The first Epistle he wrote says, "That which was from the beginning...the Word of life." Revelation also says, "The things which you have seen...and the things which are about to take place after these things." John wrote "from the beginning" all the way to "forever and ever." There was no decline at all in the life of the aged John. Therefore, our old age need not be days of deterioration. The history of Solomon's old age (1 Kings 11:1-8) should not be the history of our old age. God shows us that our old age should be days of fullness. Even though David sinned, his ending was better than his beginning; he ended by preparing for the building of the temple. Although Peter denied the Lord three times, in the end he was for the Lord. Although Mark once withdrew from the work because of difficulty (Acts 13:13; 15:37-38), he still wrote the Gospel according to Mark, and eventually he was profitable to Paul for the ministry (2 Tim. 4:11). The histories of these men show us that they all did very well in the last stretch of their journey.

Let us come back to Jacob. In the beginning he was crafty and deceitful to the uttermost, yet in the end he was transformed into a lovely person, a useful person in God's hand. If we compare Jacob with Isaac and Abraham, we may say that Jacob's ending was better than that of Abraham and much better than that of Isaac. The shining in Jacob's later years comes almost as a surprise to us. We may think that a person like Jacob is without much hope and not worthy of being perfected. Even if he improved, we may think that he would not end up being of much use in God's hand. But individually speaking, Abraham's and Isaac's endings were not as good as Jacob's. Both Abraham's and Isaac's later years seem a little rusty. However, Jacob's later years were shining and fruitful. God was able to accomplish in him in his later years all that was absent in his early years. Let us look at some of the events in Jacob's later years.

THE QUIET JACOB

Beginning from Genesis 37 Jacob withdrew; he retired. Before this time Jacob was active from morning until evening. As soon as he was finished with one matter, he would become involved in another matter. Jacob typified the strength of the flesh. No one could stop Jacob from his activity or his speaking. At Peniel God touched him. At Bethel God perfected him. At Hebron Jacob withdrew to the background. Beginning from chapter thirty-seven, he only occasionally came forward to speak a few words or to take care of something. Most of the time he retreated to the background. He became quiet.

If we know Jacob, we will realize that his natural energy would not allow him to rest. Some Christians are like this. If you ask them to rest for a couple of days, they simply cannot do it. They do not know how to stop. However, Jacob was quiet in his later years. He was no longer active in his natural life.

This was the fruit of the Spirit in Jacob. This does not mean that after our natural life has been dealt with, we will become a lazy person; nor does it mean that a person who seldom endeavors is necessarily one that dwells in Hebron. If we think that being spiritual is doing very little or even doing nothing, we are very wrong. When we say that Jacob was quiet, we mean that Jacob's natural energy stopped. After Jacob returned to his father's house to dwell in Hebron, he became quiet and retreated. The work of the Spirit prevailed in Jacob.

The most outstanding characteristic of a person whose flesh has been dealt with by God is the cessation of fleshly activities. Even an energetic person such as Jacob can become quiet and inactive. There is nothing to marvel at when a lazy person retreats to the background. The Lord may deal with such a person by pushing him to the foreground. However, Jacob was a person who was always active, always asserting himself in the forefront. His retreat to the background was truly the result of God's work on him.

We know that Jacob was a crafty, cunning, and scheming person. This kind of person does not usually have any concern for others. It is difficult to find a scheming person who truly loves others. A person who always plots against others has only one goal—to profit at the expense of others. He will do whatever profits him and not do anything that does not profit him. He can never sympathize with others or be considerate of others. He can never love others. This was Jacob. Jacob's nature was one that only cared for himself. He did not know how to love others. Even his love for Rachel was a selfish love. Yet God disciplined him. After he left his father's house, he endured much suffering and encountered many difficulties. When he returned to his father's house, his loved ones passed away one by one. His daughter, Dinah, was defiled, and his eldest son, Reuben, defiled his bed. Jacob's sufferings were really great. By the time he settled in Hebron he had lost everything. Yet through all these sufferings, he gradually became mature. He was no longer active in himself; rather, he became quiet and retreated to the background.

THE COMPASSIONATE JACOB

Jacob began to turn into a compassionate person. When his sons were feeding the flock away from home, he sent Joseph to inquire after them. Here we see that he was an elderly person who loved and cared for the young ones. He was afraid that his sons might get into mischief, and he sent Joseph to inquire after their welfare. He never expected that Joseph would be sold or that his sons would deceive him by showing him Joseph's many-colored coat dipped in blood. Genesis 37:33 says, "And he knew it, and said, It is my son's coat; an evil beast hath devoured him; Joseph is without doubt rent in pieces." What a great sorrow this was for an old man to repeat, "Joseph is without doubt rent in pieces." The next verses say, "And Jacob rent his clothes, and put sackcloth upon his loins, and mourned for his son many days. And all his sons and all his daughters rose up to comfort him; but he refused to be comforted; and he said, For I will go down into the grave unto my son mourning. Thus his father wept for him" (vv. 34-35). Step by step God took everything away from Jacob; step by step Jacob was stripped. Even Joseph was taken from him. The record in the latter part of Genesis 37 is truly sad and sorrowful. Once again Jacob was disciplined and tried in God's hand. God was making Jacob a person full of compassion and sympathy for others.

THE TENDER JACOB

Later, Joseph was made lord over Pharaoh's house and governor over all the land of Egypt. Jacob, on the other hand, was facing famine in the land of Canaan. When Jacob was faced with this calamity, he sent his sons to buy corn in Egypt. Benjamin, his youngest son, did not go. While his sons were buying food in Egypt, Joseph recognized them. Joseph purposely detained Simeon. He would release him on the condition that they bring Benjamin to him. When the sons returned home, they told Jacob all that had befallen them, and Jacob said to them, "Me have ye bereaved of my children: Joseph is not, and Simeon is not, and ye will take Benjamin away: all these things are against me" (Gen. 42:36). Here we

see a tender Jacob, not the Jacob of his former days. Here was
a man who lived under God's hand, whose natural life disap-
peared day by day. Before God he was transformed into a
tender and loving person.

When the corn that had been brought from Egypt was
eaten, they could go and buy food only according to the condition laid out by the governor in Egypt: They had to bring
Benjamin with them. Jacob had no other way but to let his
most treasured, youngest son go. At this point the Bible
records, "And their father Israel said unto them, If it must be
so..." (Gen. 43:11). Here the Bible calls his name Israel. The
phrase "if it must be so" indicates that he was now a tender
person; he was no longer a stubborn person. Formerly, he did
whatever he wished, but no longer. His words, "if it must be so
now, do this," indicate that Jacob was now softened and was
able to listen to others. "Take of the best fruits in the land in
your vessels, and carry down the man a present, a little balm,
and a little honey, spices and myrrh, nuts and almonds." The
aged man was now full of kindness. "And take double money
in your hand; and the money that was brought again in the
mouth of your sacks, carry it again in your hand; peradventure it was an oversight" (v. 12). He wanted to return the
money that was taken before. This was unlike his past when
he took the possessions of others as his own. "Take also your
brother, and arise, go again unto the man" (v. 13). He agreed
to let Benjamin go, saying, "And God Almighty give you mercy
before the man, that he may send away your other brother,
and Benjamin. If I be bereaved of my children, I am bereaved"
(v. 14). This Jacob was entirely different from the former
Jacob. God was taking away his most treasured son; his youngest son, Benjamin, had to leave him! In spite of all his life's
labor, he had nothing left. This was God's stripping. He said,
"If I be bereaved of my children, I am bereaved." He seemed to
be saying, "I only have one desire: May God Almighty, the
God I knew at Bethel, give you mercy before that man, and
deliver your other brother and Benjamin home." Brothers and
sisters, if you read Jacob's history as an outsider, you may not
understand him, but if you put yourself in Jacob's situation
and read his history, you will realize what kind of person

Jacob was by this time. Formerly he was a capable, cunning, and supplanting person, but now he had been transformed into a soft, tender, and loving person. How much work must God have done on him!

THE SHINING JACOB

All the above is not enough to reveal Jacob's shining brightness. From this point on, Jacob became shining. When his sons returned from Egypt the second time and told him, "Joseph is yet alive, and he is governor over all the land of Egypt," Jacob's heart fainted because he did not believe them (Gen. 45:26). Later when he saw the wagons which Joseph had sent to carry him, his spirit revived, and "Israel said, It is enough; Joseph my son is yet alive: I will go and see him before I die" (v. 28). We need to note when the Bible calls him Jacob and when it calls him Israel. He was already a tender person. If he had been the Jacob of twenty or forty years earlier, he probably would have severely scolded his sons under such circumstances. He might have said, "Why have you cheated me for so long?" But he only said, "It is enough;... I will go and see him before I die." Here we touch gentleness, maturity, and a character refined by fire. Within Jacob there was the constitution of the Holy Spirit which could not be found in the former Jacob.

Although Jacob said, "I will go and see him," a question rose up within him. It seems as if he was asking, "Can I really go down to Egypt? Can I truly go down to Egypt for Joseph's sake? My grandfather, Abraham, sinned while going down to Egypt. He was reproached and he returned. My father Isaac wanted to go down to Egypt when he met famine, but God appeared and warned him that he should not go down to Egypt. He obeyed God's commandment, and God blessed him. Now can I, who have inherited the promises of Abraham and Isaac, go down to Egypt because of Joseph? Joseph is my beloved, and he is governor over Egypt and cannot come to me, but is this natural tie of father and son enough reason for me to go down to Egypt? If I go down to Egypt, what will happen to God's commandment? What will happen to God's promises? What will become of this land, God's inheritance?

Will this lineage be frustrated if I go down to Egypt? How will the line of Abraham and Isaac be consummated?" This was a problem. Jacob was afraid to be wrong in himself. Therefore, when he came to Beer-sheba, he stopped and offered sacrifices to God (Gen. 46:1).

For the first time, Jacob shone more brightly than he ever did before. When he sent Benjamin to Joseph, he said, "God Almighty give you mercy before the man, that he may send away your other brother, and Benjamin." This revealed a condition in him that had not been present before. Now he thought of God's promises, God's plan, God's inheritance, and God's covenant. He became fearful; therefore, he rose up unto Beer-sheba "and offered sacrifices unto the God of his father Isaac." This shows that he was entirely different from before. He offered sacrifices and seemed to say to God, "I am here to serve You; all that I have is on the altar. It is fine with me whether I go or not. This is the position that I am standing on before You." If we look at what God said to him in the following passage, we can know Jacob's feeling at the time. "And God spake unto Israel in the visions of the night, and said, Jacob, Jacob. And he said, Here am I. And he said, I am God, the God of thy father: fear not to go down into Egypt" (vv. 2-3). This proves that Jacob was fearful. Thank God, this fearfulness reveals what God had done in him. Jacob's concern about whether or not he could go down to Egypt for the sake of Joseph shows that he had attained what Abraham and Isaac had not attained. Abraham went down to Egypt on his own when he faced famine. Isaac also wanted to go down to Egypt when he met famine, but fortunately God stopped him. But here was a man whom God did not stop. Jacob stopped halfway by himself. He thought of God's promises and God's covenant and became fearful. What should he do? He could do only one thing: offer up sacrifices to God. The altar was the place for him. He waited until God said to him, "Fear not to go down into Egypt; for I will there make of thee a great nation. I will go down with thee into Egypt; and I will also surely bring thee up again." At that word he dared to rise up from Beer-sheba. This was the constitution of the Holy Spirit! He was another person, totally different from what he had been before. Inside this person was the constitution, establishment, and testimony of the Spirit.

THE JACOB WHO KEPT HIS STANDING

He came to Egypt, saw Joseph, and settled in the land of Goshen. Then Joseph presented him unto Pharaoh. Genesis 47:7 says, "And Joseph brought in Jacob his father, and set him before Pharaoh: and Jacob blessed Pharaoh." What a beautiful picture! Although Jacob was the father of the governor, humanly speaking, he was still a little lower than Pharaoh. Jacob was also a man fleeing from famine, a refugee. He came to the land of Pharaoh to look to Pharaoh for his food and his living. How much he needed to rely on Pharaoh! If this had been the former Jacob, what would he have done upon meeting Pharaoh? When he met his own brother, he humbly addressed him as "my lord" and referred to himself as "your servant." When he came to the king of Egypt, should he not have been even more flattering to Pharaoh? But he was totally different. Upon entering, he blessed Pharaoh. Hebrews 7:7 says, "But without any dispute the lesser is blessed by the greater." Jacob did not have a sense that he was a refugee, a man fleeing from famine. He was not affected by Pharaoh's high and great position. Although Egypt was the strongest country at that time and Pharaoh was the king of this great country, as well as Jacob's benefactor, Jacob did not lose his standing in the presence of Pharaoh. Although to the world, Pharaoh's position was high, Jacob knew that there was nothing lofty about it spiritually. Therefore, Jacob could bless Pharaoh. Jacob kept his spiritual standing. "And Pharaoh said unto Jacob, How old art thou? And Jacob said unto Pharaoh, The days of the years of my pilgrimage are a hundred and thirty years: few and evil have the days of the years of my life been, and have not attained unto the days of the years of the life of my fathers in the days of their pilgrimage" (Gen. 47:8-9). Jacob spoke with much feeling: "Few and evil have the days of the years of my life been, and have not attained unto the days of the years of the life of my fathers." He knew his own condition. He did not feel that he was great and capable at all. "And Jacob blessed Pharaoh" (v. 10). Before he left he blessed Pharaoh again. When we read this we can only say that Jacob was a lovable person.

By nature, Jacob was an emulous, selfish, and covetous person. Now in Egypt, having blessed Pharaoh and having the governor as his son, he had a good opportunity to gain recognition from Pharaoh and his son. But he did not do this. Just as the aged Jacob retreated to the background in the land of Canaan, he stepped back in Egypt. During those years, Jacob receded to the background in a simple way. If he had been the former Jacob, we do not know what he would have done with such a good opportunity. Previously, he looked for ways even when he had no way. When he met the miserly Laban, he could still find ways to squeeze something out of him. However, those days were gone. Jacob was not Jacob any longer. He had become Israel.

We must read the history of Jacob in his later years in the light of his condition in his early years. In the early years he was busy and calculating. But in his later years he did not speak much, and he was not active. He was the Israel who had receded to the background. This was the work of God. Many times, God's greatest work consists of stopping us from our own activity, speaking, and proposals. God had completed His work in Jacob. Therefore, we now find Jacob saying nothing, doing nothing, and being stripped of everything.

"SHINETH MORE AND MORE UNTO THE PERFECT DAY"

Jacob lived in Egypt for seventeen years. His days on earth were coming to an end. During the time he lived in the land of Goshen, not much happened to him; he just lived a simple life. However, he did not become rusty during those seventeen years; he was progressing all the time. Day by day he shone brighter and brighter. Indeed he shone more and more unto the perfect day. His death marked the time of the zenith of his shining. We pray that God would give us an ending similar to his.

Genesis 47:28-30 says, "And Jacob lived in the land of Egypt seventeen years: so the whole age of Jacob was a hundred forty and seven years. And the time drew nigh that Israel must die: and he called his son Joseph, and said unto him, If now I have found grace in thy sight, put, I pray thee, thy hand under my thigh, and deal kindly and truly with me; bury me not, I pray thee, in Egypt: but I will lie with my fathers, and thou shalt carry me out of Egypt, and bury me in their buryingplace. And he said, I will do as thou hast said."

It is interesting to note that while Jacob was in the land of Egypt, he never told his son what kind of dwelling or living he wanted. But now he said to his son, "I will lie with my fathers, and thou shalt carry me out of Egypt, and bury me in their buryingplace." He did not care about eating and clothing in the land of Egypt. He was not bothered by these things. He accepted whatever his son gave him. However, regarding his burial place after his death, he was very particular because this was related to God's promise, the land of God's promise, and the kingdom God would establish. Previously, Jacob was a man who only cared for his own profit. However, now he was not concerned about personal comfort, but about the covenant between God and His house, that is, the position which Abraham, Isaac, and Jacob occupied in God's testimony. The former Jacob was a crafty person who upbraided his sons Simeon and Levi. The present Jacob mildly called his son Joseph to come. Previously, when Joseph told Jacob about his dream of the sun, moon, and eleven stars bowing down to him, Jacob rebuked him and said to him, "Shall I and thy mother and thy brethren indeed come to bow down ourselves to thee to the earth?" (Gen. 37:10). Now he called his son and gently, not disapprovingly, said, "If now I have found grace in thy sight..." This man was indeed mature. He said, "Put, I pray thee, thy hand under my thigh, and deal kindly and truly with me; bury me not, I pray thee, in Egypt." He uttered the most important things with the most tender words. He said, "But I will lie with my fathers, and thou shalt carry me out of Egypt, and bury me in their buryingplace." These words show us that God had constituted a new character in Jacob.

The following words are very precious: "And Israel bowed himself upon the bed's head" (v. 31). "Upon the bed's head" corresponds to "leaning on the top of his staff," which is quoted in the book of Hebrews (11:21). We believe that since the time he became lame he carried a staff. On the one hand, the staff spoke of his lameness. On the other hand, it indicated that he was a sojourner. Now he worshipped God while leaning on the top of his staff. By this he was saying to God, "Everything that You have done with me is the best that could be. Therefore, I worship You."

In chapter forty-eight he became sick, and Joseph brought his two sons to visit him. Jacob said to Joseph, "God Almighty appeared unto me at Luz in the land of Canaan, and blessed me, and said unto me, Behold, I will make thee fruitful, and multiply thee, and I will make of thee a multitude of people; and will give this land to thy seed after thee for an everlasting possession" (vv. 3-4). He recognized God's name as "God Almighty." He did not remember how he competed with his brother, how he gained the birthright, or how he took his brother's blessing, etc. All he remembered was his relationship with God.

He continued to say, "And now thy two sons, Ephraim and Manasseh, which were born unto thee in the land of Egypt, before I came unto thee into Egypt, are mine; as Reuben and Simeon, they shall be mine. And thy issue, which thou begettest after them, shall be thine, and shall be called after the name of their brethren in their inheritance. And as for me, when I came from Padan, Rachel died by me in the land of Canaan in the way, when yet there was but a little way to come unto Ephrath: and I buried her there in the way of Ephrath; the same is Bethlehem" (vv. 5-7). These were the things he remembered. Here we touch his person. We see his attitude toward God and his attitude before men. This shows us clearly that he was now a different person, one with feeling and tenderness.

"And Israel beheld Joseph's sons, and said, Who are these? And Joseph said unto his father, They are my sons, whom God hath given me in this place. And he said, Bring them, I pray thee, unto me, and I will bless them" (vv. 8-9). When he blessed Joseph's two sons, he laid his right hand on Ephraim's head and his left hand on Manasseh's head. Although Ephraim was the younger and Manasseh was the firstborn, Israel laid his right hand on the head of the younger one and his left hand on the head of the firstborn, reversing the order. When

Joseph saw this, he said, "Not so, my father." What did Israel say? He said, "I know it, my son, I know it." This shows us that Jacob knew what Isaac did not know; he was clearer than Isaac. When Isaac blessed his younger son, he was deceived into blessing him, but Israel was clear about what he was doing when he blessed Joseph's younger son. Both Isaac's and Israel's eyes were dim because of age, but Israel's inner eyes were not dim. Israel said, "I know it, my son, I know it." He knew that God wanted to set Ephraim before Manasseh, that God wanted the older one to serve the younger. Here was a man who had entered into God's thoughts. Here was a man who had fellowshipped with God to such an extent and who had known God to such an extent that he could overcome the weakness of his body. What his physical eyes could not see, his inner eyes could see. The shining of Israel had indeed reached the zenith!

After giving the blessing, he showed them that Egypt was not their home. "And Israel said unto Joseph, Behold, I die; but God shall be with you, and bring you again unto the land of your fathers" (v. 21). He was saying, "Although you are prospering in Egypt, Egypt is only a place where you sojourn. We have God's purpose and God's promise, and we are God's people. After I die, God will be with you to lead you back to Canaan. You must reach God's purpose."

At the end, Jacob gathered his sons together to tell them the things that would happen to them in the future. In prophesying concerning his twelve sons, he touched incidents of their past. It was not easy for him to speak this way because as he talked about their past, it reminded him of his own past. A son more or less bears the resemblance of his father. Therefore, when Jacob spoke of his sons' weaknesses, evil, and uncleanness, it was like speaking about himself. Jacob's words concerning his sons' past were actually descriptions of his own past. What he said about his sons' future was not all that positive. Nevertheless, his speaking was compassionate and full of kindness.

We only need to consider one thing to find out the great difference between this person and the Jacob of the past. When Simeon and Levi slew all the males in the city because of the incident with Dinah, Jacob said to Simeon and Levi, "Ye have troubled me to make me to stink among the inhabitants of the land, among the Canaanites and the Perizzites: and I being few in number, they shall gather themselves together against me, and slay me; and I shall be destroyed, I and my house" (Gen. 34:30). This was what he said at Shechem. But now he mentioned it in another way: "Simeon and Levi are brethren; instruments of cruelty are in their habitations. O my soul, come not thou into their secret; unto their assembly, mine honor, be not thou united: for in their anger they slew a man, and in their self-will they digged down a wall. Cursed be their anger, for it was fierce; and their wrath, for it was cruel" (49:5-7). What he saw now was not related to his personal interests but to sin and evil. Previously, he focused on self-profit, gains, and losses. He thought, "What shall we do if the race of Shechem rises up and takes revenge on us for what you have done?" But now, he said, "Come not thou into their secret." This means that he could not take part in such slaying and killing, that such cruelty was to be cursed. Here we see a new Jacob, one who was washed, pure, and new. He possessed a new character which he did not have before.

"Dan shall judge his people, as one of the tribes of Israel. Dan shall be a serpent by the way, an adder in the path, that biteth the horse heels, so that his rider shall fall backward" (vv. 16-17). His prophecy concerning Dan's future was not that good; Dan would be serpentine in every respect and much rebellion would come out of him. At this point he immediately said, "I have waited for thy salvation, O Lord" (v. 18). He meant, "I cannot do anything about this kind of rebellion; I can only wait for God's salvation." These words reveal his new character. While he was prophesying, he was waiting for God's salvation.

Genesis 49 contains Jacob's prophecies concerning his twelve sons. Eventually, all the prophecies regarding these twelve tribes came true. Jacob was a prophet. He had entered into and understood God's mind, and he told his sons what God would do. Jacob knew more than Abraham and Isaac. He was able to foretell the things that would happen to

Manasseh, Ephraim, and the twelve tribes. This proves that he was a man who fellowshipped and communicated with God.

Jacob was a hopeless person in his early years, but God nevertheless made a vessel out of him. He made a vessel out of the cunning, scheming, and self-willed Jacob. The more we read about Jacob's later years, the more we sense his loveliness. Here was a man who was broken by God. Here was the constitution of the Holy Spirit. This was the result of God's work on him step by step. We can only say that our God is full of wisdom, grace, and patience. He will always finish His work.

After Jacob finished his prophecies, the Bible records, "All these are the twelve tribes of Israel" (v. 28). By the time Jacob was dying, the twelves tribes were formed; God's people was formed. Brothers and sisters, today God is also after a group of people to be His vessel to accomplish His purpose. Through such a group of people, all the nations on the earth will be blessed. What God did through Israel typifies what God wants to do through the church. The commission of the church is to accomplish the work of God's recovery. The church is God's vessel in His recovery work. To be the vessel in God's recovery work, the church needs to know the God of Abraham, the God of Isaac, and the God of Jacob. This does not mean that we need someone to be an Abraham, an Isaac, and a Jacob separately. It means that we must all know the God of Abraham, the God of Isaac, and the God of Jacob. After we have known Him, we will become His vessel to accomplish His purpose.

We must never be satisfied with a little spiritual experience. The Word of God tells us that God wants us to be experienced in three aspects: in knowing the Father as Abraham did, in enjoying God as Isaac did, and in being disciplined by God as Jacob was. All these three are definite experiences and definite knowledge; they are not doctrines or letters. God intends to give us the vision, the revelation, and the discipline of the Holy Spirit so that He can lead us on step by step until we become the vessel for the accomplishment of His purpose. May God give us the grace to have such a clear vision.

CHAPTER TWELVE

THE CONSTITUTION OF THE SPIRIT

Scripture Reading: Heb. 12:5-7, 9-11; Gal. 5:22-23; 4:19; 1 Cor. 3:12, 14; Gen. 2:12; Phil. 4:11-12

The title "the God of Jacob" implies how the Holy Spirit disciplined Jacob, how He dealt with Jacob's natural life, how He constituted Christ into Jacob, and how He bore the fruit of the Spirit in Jacob. If we want to know the God of Jacob, we have to know the constitution by the Spirit and the fruit of the Spirit. If we want to know the God of Jacob, we need to allow the Spirit to perform His work in us, to deal with our natural life, to constitute Christ into our inward being, and to bring forth the fruit of the Spirit in us so that we can become the vessels of God's testimony.

God deals with our natural life for the purpose of ushering us into the carving work of the Spirit, the processing by the Spirit, and the constituting of the Spirit. What is the meaning of constitution? The constitution referred to here is a vertical and horizontal interweaving of knitwork. The constitution of the Spirit means that the Spirit constitutes Christ into our being to the point that we and Christ become one. Therefore, the constitution of the Spirit is one step more advanced than Christ being our life. Christ being our life is the foundation; the Spirit constituting Christ into our being is maturity. Christ being our life is Christ within us living for us. The constitution of the Spirit is the constituting of Christ into us to the extent that Christ's character becomes our character. God's goal in dealing with our natural life is that we would have the constitution of the Spirit. The knowledge of the God of Isaac is a knowledge of the God who has given Christ to us for our enjoyment. The knowledge of the God of Jacob is the knowledge of the Spirit who is constituting Christ into our being. This condition is like the weaving and constituting of an embroidery work.

PARTAKING OF GOD'S HOLINESS

Hebrews 12:9-10 says, "The Father of spirits...disciplined...for what is profitable that we might partake of His holiness." God deals with us and the Spirit works in us step by step, leading us through many hardships and distressing situations for the purpose of making us partakers of "His holiness." "His holiness" here is not the "sanctification" spoken of in 1 Corinthians 1:30. The sanctification in 1 Corinthians 1 is a matter of Christ being our sanctification; Christ is made sanctification to us. Hebrews 12 speaks of the Father of spirits who takes us through disciplines and trials so that we may partake of His holiness. Such a holiness is produced through our trials. It is wrought out of discipline and produced by the Spirit through all the difficult and adverse environments we encounter. "Now no discipline at the present time seems to be a matter of joy, but of grief; but afterward it yields the peaceable fruit of righteousness to those who have been exercised by it" (Heb. 12:11). This is the result of the work of the Holy Spirit in us.

The natural life of some Christians is inclined to exhibition. They are like Hezekiah, who was fond of showing off all that he had to others (2 Kings 20:12-13). When God heals them of a particular kind of sickness, they incessantly "testify" of this matter to others. Actually this is not testifying, but idle talking, and the particular sickness often returns because these people are prone to show themselves off; therefore, God has to discipline them. When they eventually become tired of their exhibition, they will spontaneously stop their bragging "testimonies." They will not need to grit their teeth and make up their minds to not brag anymore. They will have been dealt with by God to such an extent that the peaceable fruit has been produced spontaneously, and they no longer act the way they once did. This is the constitution of the Spirit. God has not only given Christ to us to be our life, but He is constituting Christ into our being to be our character. Christ being our life is the foundation, while the nature of Christ becoming our nature is the constitution of the Spirit. The Spirit deals with our natural life with the purpose of producing a new character in us. God uses all kinds of ways to discipline us so that we may partake of His holiness and bring forth the peaceable fruit of righteousness.

This is what the history of Jacob shows. Jacob not only knew that God is the beginning of everything and the strength behind everything; he also acquired a new character. God worked on him and constituted Christ's character into him so that Christ's character became his character. In his later years, Jacob was entirely changed because Christ's character was constituted into him.

THE FRUIT OF THE SPIRIT

Galatians 5:22-23 says, "But the fruit of the Spirit is love, joy, peace, longsuffering, kindness, goodness, faithfulness, meekness, self-control." This shows us that "love, joy, peace, longsuffering, kindness, goodness, faithfulness, meekness, self-control" are not virtues given to us by the Holy Spirit, but are fruit borne by the Holy Spirit in us. The fruit of the Holy Spirit means that something of Christ is assimilated by us through the work of the Holy Spirit with the result that these things become our character and our characteristics. This is the meaning of the fruit of the Spirit. This is what we mean when we say that the Holy Spirit is constituting Christ into us. The Holy Spirit is doing one work in us, which is to deal with our natural life and to constitute Christ in us, making Christ's character our character so that spontaneously "love, joy, peace, longsuffering, kindness, goodness, faithfulness, meekness, self-control" will be lived out of us and we will bear the fruit of the Spirit. This is what God is showing us today.

CHRIST BEING FORMED IN US

Paul told the Galatians that he travailed "again in birth until Christ is formed in you" (Gal. 4:19). God has given Christ to the believers; this is the first step. But He wants to do a deeper work, which is to have Christ formed in us. God deals with our natural life so that Christ may be formed in us, that is, that Christ may be wrought into us and constituted in us.

Peter was originally a very strong person. His natural life always put him ahead of others. After God touched his natural life, that is, after He touched his strongest part, Peter became weak. However, Peter's weakness was not the end. God went on to constitute Christ into his being. As a result, when others touched Peter, they realized that his being was changed and that he had become a new person. What is the extent of the work of the Spirit? He works to the extent that Christ is constituted and formed in us.

Paul said in Philippians 4:11, "I have learned." This was Christ being formed in him, which he learned step by step. He learned "how to be abased" and "how to abound;" he learned "in whatever circumstances…to be content." "In everything and in all things I have learned the secret" (v. 12). Paul's person had undergone a basic change. Therefore, not only do we need Christ in us to be our life, but we also need Christ to be formed in us. Not only do we have the Christ given to us by God, but we also need the Christ assimilated by us and then formed in us. This is what God wants us to attain. This is to know the God of Jacob.

THE FORMING OF PRECIOUS STONES

We need to pay special attention to three portions of the Scripture. One portion is Genesis 2, where gold and precious stones are mentioned. Another portion is 1 Corinthians 3, where gold and precious stones are built upon a foundation. The third portion is Revelation 21, which speaks of the New Jerusalem being composed of pure gold, and the foundations of the wall of the city being adorned with every precious stone. God's purpose is not only with gold and silver, but also with precious stones. We know that gold typifies God the Father. All that is of God is gold. Silver signifies redemption, typifying the Son. All the gifts of Christ are silver. How about the precious stones? The precious stones are not like gold and silver, which are elements. They are compounds of several elements. Precious stones are formed through the process of intense underground heat. Continuous heat brings about a chemical change, and precious stones are formed. Only after the stones are carved, cut, and polished do they become beautiful and valuable gems. Therefore, the precious stones typify the work of the Holy Spirit in man. Day by day the Spirit works on us, carves us, deals with us, and constitutes us until Christ is formed in us. The Spirit leads us through many difficulties and environments so that Christ may be constituted into our being. When Christ in us becomes not only the Christ given by God, but the Christ digested and assimilated into us, we become the precious stones.

In Genesis 2 there is gold and there are the precious stones, but there is no silver. According to God's eternal plan, this signifies that everything comes out of Him and that the Holy Spirit constitutes Christ into us. Silver signifies the Christ that God has given to us; yet this alone is not enough. God wants Christ to be constituted into us, that is, to be digested and assimilated by us and formed in us until we become precious stones. In the new heaven and new earth, God will reach His goal, and there will be only gold and precious stones, but no silver. All the silver will have become precious stones. Hence, God's ultimate goal is to have precious stones. Consequently, in Genesis 2 God used the fruit of the tree of life to signify the life that He gives to us. Fruit is something that is eaten and digested. God not only wants to give us life; He also wants us to digest life.

May God open our eyes to see that in His holy way and according to His plan, He wants to gain some vessels to fulfill His goal. These vessels must know the God of Abraham; they must know that all things are of God. They must also know the God of Isaac; they must know that everything for our enjoyment and inheritance is given to us by Him. They must know that everything depends on our being in Christ and Christ being in us. They must also know the God of Jacob; they must know that God deals with our natural life and constitutes Christ into our being through the Spirit. May God bless us, and may He lead us to the knowledge of the God of Abraham, the God of Isaac, and the God of Jacob so that we may become vessels for His testimony.